"With bravery, Anne and Nelson Smith served our country. With even more pronounced bravery, they share their story of serving the Lord and one another in marriage. Their heartache rings true for so many of God's children and it is my prayer that Anne's example of reliance on the Lord strengthens the spirits of women and girls in Virginia and across the world—promoting light and life in the midst of dark valleys and seemingly insurmountable challenges."

—Suzanne S. Youngkin, First Lady of Virginia

"Anne is definitely an incredible woman, but it's clearly Christ in her that has brought the kind of peace that transcends the deepest losses and trials in our marriages. Her transformational words, hard-won and true, are an invitation to receive the deep hope and joy available when we finally let God lead us through life's good/hard dance."

—Katherine Wolf, author, *Treasures in the Dark,*
Suffer Strong, and *Hope Heals*

"*Recalibrated* is a resource I wish I had had forty years ago, when as a newly married rookie police officer I began the challenges of married life within the world of crime and punishment. It took years to find grace and beauty and safety in the bond of marriage. Anne's brave story provides a hopeful path forward through what might seem a dark road."

—Jamie Winship, cofounder, Identity Exchange; author, *Living Fearless*

"I remember the first time I met Nelson like it was yesterday, though it was more than ten years ago. He walked into my windowless battalion chaplain's office (located near the 5th SFG HQ at Fort Campbell, KY) asking me if we could talk about spiritual matters. I did not see him often; but whenever he was in my office, I would end up spending well over an hour listening (to him and the Holy Spirit), advising him, and praying for him. I knew his PTSD was creating waves in his marriage, but I did not know that those waves were tsunami-sized ones. As I was reading about Anne's experience of 'walking through the valley of the shadow of death' during the early years of their marriage and finally being led to 'green pastures' by 'still waters' (Psalm 23), I found myself saying a loud *amen* and *alleluia* to our gracious heavenly Father who brings life wherever there is death. In addition to causing a reader to better understand what many of our nation's combat veterans and their spouses go through, this book will create an urge to pray to and worship the God who gives 'beauty for ashes, the oil of joy for mourning' (Isaiah 61:3)."

—Seung-Il Suh, United States Army chaplain

"In *Recalibrated*, Anne W. Smith shares a raw and transparent story of her marriage to a Green Beret combat veteran grappling with PTSD and the destructive communication patterns that kept them trapped in pain and hopelessness. Her candid narrative provides an intimate look into their personal journey and their clinical process while emphasizing the power of surrendering to God in the face of seemingly insurmountable challenges. While many observers (and clinicians) would have pronounced this marriage without hope of surviving, the author shares with deep vulnerability how their dependence on God led to transformation and flourishing. This book is a testimony to the strength of faith and the miracles that can happen despite horrific trauma and woundedness when we let go and let God take the lead. There is nothing beyond His reach that can't be healed, restored, and redeemed!"

—Lisa Rattner, LCSW, Christian
Counseling & Coaching, PLLC

RECALIBRATED

HOW A GREEN BERET AND HIS BRIDE OVERCAME REALITIES
OF COMBAT AND A BROKEN RELATIONSHIP THROUGH
FAITH, HOPE, & LOVE.

*Encouragement to find the
light at the end of
every valley —*

Anne W. Smith

Anne W. Smith

WESTBOW
PRESS®
A DIVISION OF THOMAS NELSON
& ZONDERVAN

Scripture quotations marked NIV are taken from the Holy Bible, New International Version®, NIV®. Copyright © 1973, 1978, 1984 by Biblica, Inc.™ Used by permission of Zondervan. All rights reserved worldwide.

Scripture quotations marked NLT are taken from the Holy Bible, New Living Translation, copyright © 1996, 2004, 2007 by Tyndale House Foundation. Used by permission of Tyndale House Publishers, Inc., Carol Stream, Illinois 60188. All rights reserved.

Mere Christianity by C.S. Lewis copyright ©1942, 1943, 1944, 1952 C.S. Lewis Pte. Ltd. The Voyage of the Dawn Treader by C.S. Lewis copyright © 1952 C.S. Lewis Pte. Ltd. Extracts reprinted by permission.

WestBow Press books may be ordered through booksellers or by contacting:

WestBow Press
A Division of Thomas Nelson & Zondervan
1663 Liberty Drive
Bloomington, IN 47403
www.westbowpress.com
844-714-3454

Because of the dynamic nature of the Internet, any web addresses or links contained in this book may have changed since publication and may no longer be valid. The views expressed in this work are solely those of the author and do not necessarily reflect the views of the publisher, and the publisher hereby disclaims any responsibility for them.

Any people depicted in stock imagery provided by Getty Images are models, and such images are being used for illustrative purposes only. Certain stock imagery © Getty Images.

ISBN: 979-8-3850-3018-7 (sc)
ISBN: 979-8-3850-3019-4 (hc)
ISBN: 979-8-3850-3020-0 (e)

Library of Congress Control Number: 2024915227

Print information available on the last page.

WestBow Press rev. date: 09/20/2024

CONTENTS

Contents

FOREWORD

When I first met Anne in a small group we were both a part of, her calm demeanor brought me peace. She seemed grounded and centered, and she was passionate about the Spirit of God. She was as full of adventure as she was poise, and I hung on every word of her tales of her previous peace-building work with Taliban leaders.

Nelson, her husband, was full of confidence, grit, and survival stories from Iraq as a Green Beret. My husband, Matthew, and I loved listening to them reminisce about their time in the Middle East. Both working and leading an organization working in war zones, we were drawn to their war stories but, more importantly, we were drawn to their hearts.

Unknowingly, we met them in the middle of inner turmoil, hiding the arguments, the tears, and their pleading prayers to God. What we saw on the outside was a cool couple in a small group. As most of us do, we want to hide our pain. We want to tuck it away like a bruise that we don't want anyone to see. But that was not the end of their story. By the grace of God, Anne and Nelson brought us into their underlying truths and we walked together through their dark times, supporting them as friends and in prayer.

Now ten years later, Anne's words and unique perspective on these pages brought me healing and inspiration in a difficult time. Her vulnerability helped me feel understood, and her candidness was a breath of hope. But, most importantly, her surrendered heart opened my eyes to how God could bring healing to all of us, regardless of our situation.

This book is not only about surviving actual war; it is also about surviving martial chaos. It teaches us forgiveness and humility. In time, we will all be in those places where it all seems too big and hopelessness creeps in . . . where we want to give up on a relationship—be that a spouse, a parent, or a friend.

Anne not only teaches us about the wounds of trauma, but she also teaches us about the beauty of healing, about looking in, and about looking up. She teaches us the importance of picking up our swords and fighting for love when all seems lost.

As you will read, Anne and Nelson's journey of overcoming a marriage in shambles is one of white-knuckle grit. It is a testimony of the power of surrender, humility, and reaching out for help. It shows us all how coming back to God, as our North Star, can lead us out of the trenches. One of my favorite parts of this story is that there were no miracle moments. Healing came slowly— by showing up to counseling sessions, small groups, and looking into the mirror.

This is a story of how two hopeless, broken people headed toward divorce crawled out of the pit one prayer at a time. How God took frayed edges and turned them into a tapestry for His glory. If you are close to giving up on a relationship or on yourself, read on, friend. May *Recalibrated* bring you as much healing and hope as it did for me.

—Bethany Haley Williams, PhD
Founder, Exile International; author, *The Color of Grace*

A Note from Nelson

Dear Reader,

The mind is a funny thing—capable of great and unbridled contemplation, innovation, and reasoning, yet deeply shrouded in mystery, easily deceived, and often a product of our own flawed judgments. The mind, intricately connected to will and emotions, is shaped through experiences and how we interact with the world. Perception, it is said, is reality. Most of the time this is a good and normal thing, unless perception is formed through wounded thinking and negative mindsets. The ability to question how, why, or what feeds perceptions is a uniquely human attribute, and one that is most poignant in community.

My mind and heart were bruised through the normal trials of life and also through grueling years of combat as a Green Beret. After a career in the 5th Special Forces Group that spanned seven combat deployments, countless oversees trainings, lost brothers-in-arms, and a fraught first marriage, my world fell apart. I fell apart.

The following analogy paints a picture of the transitions faced at the end of my military career:

I was the driver of a train, a really fast bullet train. I became really good at pulling the levers and pushing the buttons to make this train as efficient and fast as possible. Then one day someone tapped me on the shoulder and said it was time for me to go. I jumped off the train and rolled, tumbling, until I came to a stop. Standing up and dusting myself off, dizziness overtook me. I was completely disoriented. As I tried to make sense of where I was, I could hear the train getting quieter in the distance, and the *clickety-clack, clickety-clack* of all that I had known grew dim.

Alone in the dark, fear and uncertainty gripped me as my reality came into view. I had no idea where I was, what to do, or how to begin—and no one was there to show me or take my hand. Operating from this fear center, my instincts and perceptions took over as I desperately tried to make sense of my new reality. The adjustment was acute and demanding.

People, myself included, often think they are alone in their journey, or that their deep-rooted pain is something no else can feel or understand. The truth of the matter is, that is a lie. No snowflake is like another, yet they are all made from the same element. Such is true with humans. As unique as the Lord crafted each of us, we all contend with similar underlying struggles, pains, and hurts. My story is one of hope; hope in the fact that you can make it, you do matter, you can heal, you can recover.

Everyone has a story and I encourage you to tell your story. Do not shy away from the hurt and the pain. We are meant to be in communion with each other. That doesn't mean Instagram communion, it means bringing people into your house and showing them your dirty laundry and allowing friends to help clean, fold, and put it away. Show people you are real, and your pain may resonate, and in turn help people feel like they are not alone after jumping off their own train. There is healing in community, in honesty, in faith.

This narrative, from my wife's perspective, is hers, but it is also mine. What you are about to read is hard for me to read, to remember who I was—my brokenness and the hurt I caused. I own my past, but I am not that man anymore; through the grace and power of God, I have been redeemed. I have been recalibrated. Now my wife and I walk together through the fires and challenges of life stronger. Faith, hope, and love bind us together—not like a cliché wall ornament, but as an unshakeable foundation that adds depth, resilience, and genuine connection to our lives.

In faith, hope and love,
Nelson

OPENING THOUGHTS

Blessed be the . . . God of all comfort, who comforts us in all our affliction, so that we may be able to comfort those who are in any affliction, with the comfort with which we ourselves are comforted by God. —2 Corinthians 1:3-4

Just days after my white wedding, my world came crashing down, turning into a long, dark, desert period: a period defined by intense emotional upheaval and the stripping away of who we thought we were. Traumas of the past brought new traumas, which compounded into a caustic cocktail of emotional and verbal abuse, fear and despair.

Truly, we all carry wounds: from others, from our own choices, from things that have happened to us and around us. Wounds of the mind and heart are not flesh wounds, but soul wounds. These wounds impact every part of our lives, especially if left untreated. It is easy to diagnose broken bones or cancerous cells; it is not so easy to figure out what is wrong with the deepest part of us, our souls, how we think, why we react the ways we do, and how we perceive and interact with the world around us.

The past is powerful because it cannot be undone. Memories keep the past alive and activate us both individually and collectively toward what will become future memories. While writing my master's thesis, which was on tribalism in Iraq, I stumbled upon an account of a tribal council that described how the elders opened the council by recounting all unatoned blood feuds from their four-hundred-year history requiring *qisaas*, or "eye-for-an-eye" blood payment. Many of the feuds from centuries back had not been resolved and therefore were as poignant today as they were in the beginning. Teaching each generation the grievances of the tribe kept its history alive and relevant, regardless of how many centuries had passed. Recounting history, struggles, miracles, sorrows, you name it, has power in the present—power to ignite emotions, to weave a common bond, and to unite people.

Our story as believers is to also remember our *qisaas*, and the sacrifice that was our blood payment. It is through Jesus' blood that we are freed from revenge, from anger, bitterness, jealousy, and pride. It is only His blood that brings freedom through forgiveness. The Almighty God does not want His people, His tribe, to not forget His blessings and provisions.

> Let each generation tell its children of your mighty acts; let them proclaim your power. I will meditate on your majestic, glorious splendor and your wonderful miracles. Your awe-inspiring deeds will be on every tongue; I will proclaim your greatness. Everyone will share the story of your wonderful goodness; they will sing with joy about your righteousness. (Psalm 145: 4-7, NLT)

As sons and daughters of the Most High God we are not bound to our past. In fact, in Isaiah 43 we are commanded *not* to dwell on the hurts or grievances of the past, for God is doing new things in us. He is making streams in the wasteland. He is making us new creations! As Jesus people we dwell on the power of the blood that redeems and springs forth a river of life from within. When you meditate on the power and might and faithfulness of our God, you begin to think, *Okay, do it again, Lord. Do it again!*

Through trials, being sifted and refined, I now feel called to strengthen my brothers and sisters with the same hope and comfort I received. So here I am, retelling to you what the Lord has done to bring healing and reconciliation to a very broken marriage, and to us individually. If you are spiraling from the struggles of an overbearing relationship and overwhelming emotions, I have been in similar shoes.

My story is not everyone's story. By today's standards I should be a divorcee. I should have broken our covenant, jumped ship, saved myself. This book is neither an excuse for those who are abusive nor to encourage others to stay in an abusive relationship. As a companion walking alongside you, I am opening my heart, my journal, my raw and vulnerable past *so that* you may know there is hope. There is a God who sees, a God who cares, and a God who comforts.

A situation may seem hopeless, as mine did, but there are those who long to help, and there is a God, the God of all comfort, who pursues each of us relentlessly. My story will perhaps convince you of the power of the Living God to transform, but my husband and I both had to be willing to change.

The following chapters contain graphic scenes of war, battle, arguments, and disputes. These are Nelson's recollections; these are my impressions. This is our story. It is candid and real. But fundamentally the emphasis of this book is not the gruesome past but the hope of a future. Our story does not dwell on the brokenness, the hurt, and the pain, but tries to lead you into the presence of the One who recreates shattered jars of clay as beautiful vases. I bless your broken road, the narrow valley, and pray that from your darkness the light of Christ will shine unto a new day.

With open hands and heart,
Anne

<u>re·cal·i·brated</u>

Re—to do something again or differently

Cal·i·brate—to carefully assess, set, or adjust

Caliber—the quality of someone's character or the level of their ability

CHAPTER ONE

BEFORE THE VALLEY

"You have stolen my heart with one glance of your eyes."
—Song of Solomon 4:9

"We found love in a hopeless place."
—Rihanna

EASTER SUNDAY, 2004. BLAZING HEAT pounded the dust-coated backs of the A-Team as they rolled onto base. Hungry and tired from their mission, the men had their sights set on hot food and a hot shower. Looking up, Nelson Smith saw the commander emerge from the main building and head straight toward them. He sighed, knowing this meant rest was an illusion. There is no rest for the weary in war.

"Men, another team was just ambushed. We do not know their status. I'm sending you to help recover, assist, and bring them back," the Commander ordered. Weapons clicked and clacked as the team checked ammunition and resupplied. Opening a map on the hood of the Humvee, Nelson and his team made a hasty plan. Grabbing a candy bar for energy and extra water to stay hydrated, they loaded back up and headed south from Baghdad to the Hillah area.

1

All was quiet as they drove down the bleak monochromatic road when the sound of *ta, ta, ta* ripped open the silence, then *tink, tink* as bullets ricochetted off their armored vehicle, followed by a loud *kah boom*, as an improvised explosive device (IED) detonated between two of the vehicles. Machine-gun fire erupted; mortars started landing. Ambushed, the Special Forces convoy was being shot at from all directions. Nelson looked ahead and noticed a slight bend in the road where the highway turned to the left. This allowed the enemy to give fire from front and right. *An L-shaped ambush, a textbook ambush. We really have nowhere to go,* Nelson realized. In retrospect he commented, "You know it's a good ambush when in the middle of getting shot at you think, *Wow, this is a well-executed ambush! I'm going to die.*"

The only thing to do is fight through an ambush. Adrenaline rushing and with piercing focus, Nelson directed his drivers to "Push through! Keep driving and return fire!" Gunfire enveloped them as they moved toward it, defying the instinct to retreat. Then the air became still and quiet once again.

Breathing a deep sigh of relief, Nelson counted his men. They were all alive. The team had made it out unscathed.

Driving a little farther down the road the convoy found the team they were sent to assist. Unfortunately, the other team had been caught in the crosshairs of the same ambush and were not so fortunate. Surveying the scene, Nelson saw blood everywhere. Lots of blood. Two of their Special Forces operators had been wounded, shot through the shoulder and arm, and medecaved. "That's when I realized how much the shoulder bleeds," Nelson reflected as he recalled the pooled blood in the front seat.

The two teams linked up and returned to base without incident. Within the safety of the base, Nelson took it on himself to clean out the bloodied truck and hose it down. As he finished washing the seats, Nelson heard his name being yelled from across the courtyard. He was being summoned to a planning meeting to put together a counter response to the ambushes.

"We wanted to go and find these dudes," Nelson remembers acutely, "so along with other Special Forces units, we went back out to flank the area where we got hit." With the map back out on the front of the Humvee, the team was briefed for the third mission of the day. "There was a feeling like we were all going to die," Nelson solemnly remembers.

The chaplain came down to bid them farewell. He dropped a big box of giant-sized Baby Ruth bars on the map. "Boys, grab one. I know you're tired and you're hungry," the chaplain said. And then he prayed the Lord's protection over the men.

With the combined strength of other Special Forces units, the warriors set out to drive the route and pinpoint where the ambush had occurred, while the rescued team headed back to their base. Nelson's convoy drove up and down the highways and roads, but the insurgents did not present themselves. It seemed they had withdrawn. In fact, they had moved to a new location, a location that brought the rescued A-Team back in their crosshairs. As the rescued team drove onto their own base, bullets rang out again as a rocket-propelled grenade (RPG) ripped through one of the Humvees, instantly killing the gunner.

Nelson's convoy heard the radio messages and responded immediately, speeding toward the base of the rescued team. The base was visible in the distance as Nelson's five-vehicle convoy slowed to make a right turn. All of a sudden, Nelson saw tracers flying across the windshield, hitting an embankment of dirt on the other side.

"Contact left! Contact left," the guys on the radio yelled. "In the ravine! West side of the road!" The Special Forces operators opened up and returned fire with the 240 machine guns on the roof.

"RPG! RPG! Incoming!" the gunner screamed.

Nelson looked over to see, seemingly in slow motion, an RPG spinning in the air, heading straight for his vehicle. Opening his mouth to avoid an overpressure injury and bracing for impact, the RPG made contact.

Kur clunk. Then stillness and silence.

In a moment of God's protection, the RPG hit the top curved corner of the Humvee and bounced off, leaving only a mark and not death in its wake. As it streaked off the roof, the heat from the rocket propellant burned the uniform, neck, and face of the gunner. If the impact had been just millimeters lower, Nelson and the men in his vehicle might not have survived.

* * *

The smallest shifts in angle and sight can have enormous changes to trajectory and outcomes. This is obviously true in war and combat, but more subtly true in the calibration of our hearts and lives. The state of our hearts determines the course of our lives, our emotions, and relationships and how we see the world and interact with it. The position of our heart is most vividly revealed through marriage and committed relationships.

Marriage uncovers the deepest parts of our beings for better or for worse and forces us to contend with the realities of our hearts. Some marriages have an expiration date before the wedding vows are even spoken. Many would have deemed my marriage to be one. Every statistic was against us—it was a second marriage for my husband, there were three stepchildren and an ex-wife, we came from two different worlds, we had a whirlwind romance and married at the end of my husband's long and war-hardened career.

The earthquake of change released a tidal wave that battered us from the beginning. And we broke. But, spoiler alert! We did not stay broken. Both of us underwent the wrecking ball and the scalpel of the Most High. Through the fire of refinement, the stripping away of the old, the recalibration of the deep, we emerged in unity and strength as one.

Everyone's story is as unique as they are, but there is a commonality—hope for a future, hope for help. This is the story of how the God I serve took a helpless and hopeless situation and, through His meticulous daily presence, helped us stand, lifted our heads, and gave us renewed life. In these pages are the lessons I learned and the comfort that I pray will provide a morsel of food for thought for your own story.

Above all, this is a love story. A love story between a girl and her God, between a woman and her man, and between a covenant-keeping God and His children.

The love story started in Afghanistan.

Single, adventurous, and a heart for international conflict resolution, I was living the dream in a remote corner of northern Afghanistan. As an American civilian operating with NATO, attached to a Swedish base, I was working for peace and reconciliation through the reintegration and Commander's Emergency Response programs. My days were filled with meeting the locals, supporting the women, helping facilitate peace *shuras* and good government practices. The Taliban, however, were pushing up into the area, creating conflict, violence, and intimidation among the local tribes and villages. In response, a Special Forces Operation Detachment Alpha (ODA), or A-Team for short, was ordered to imbed in the region and support the Afghan local police. Before arriving in Afghanistan, I knew very little about the Special Forces and even less about how they operated.

United States Army Special Forces are not Rangers, they are not Seals, they are the Green Berets—highly trained military legends that take on terrorists through guerrilla and unconventional warfare. Their moto, *De Opresso Liber* (to free the oppressed), reflects their history and mission. The simple but time-tested phrase "quiet professionals" best describes their ethic and culture. Special Forces (SF) soldiers are principled, disciplined, and operate with much latitude and autonomy. The selection and qualification process to become an SF soldier weeds out the weak and unfit candidates, leaving only the sharpest, most resilient soldiers to be the refined tip of the spear in unconventional warfare. Highly rigorous physical and mental training prepares Green Berets to withstand increased levels of stress both internally and externally in all kinds of operation theaters. These men are trained to perform under pressure and survive under extraordinary circumstances. As one study shows, SF personnel are proportionally more likely to report higher levels of physical and mental functioning at baseline than general army infantrymen.[1] These are the *creme de la creme* of soldiers.

Once qualified as a Green Beret, soldiers are placed in twelve-man units called A-Teams. Each member of the team is an expert in a specialized field— medical, engineering, operations, intelligence, leadership, or weapons. Teams are extremely flexible and cross-trained, able to divide into even smaller units to leverage the full capacity of the team. Special Forces A-Teams are able to quickly adapt to changing circumstances, mission demands, and varied cultural contexts. A-Teams work with and through indigenous forces in order to achieve their missions. Teams are geographically oriented, trained to speak native languages and maintain a deep knowledge of local cultures. The A-Team assigned to my area was made up of experts in Middle Eastern and Afghan languages as well as local cultural nuances.

Special Forces, when deployed, are the men with beards, the ones who can patrol on ATVs and ride in civilian trucks, and seemed to be a big deal, especially when in a combat zone, otherwise known as "downrange." My first "sighting" of this rare breed of human was on Christmas Day in Kabul. Eating Christmas dinner of prepared turkey, stuffing, and all the fixings in a tent with hundreds of people from around the world, a hush came over the dining facility. I looked up as a team of big, burly, bearded warriors entered the dining area. Whispers quickly circulated around the room. "Hey, those guys are Special Forces." It was like Demi-gods had descended on the chow hall. In all honesty, they were the meanest, toughest, hardest-looking men in the tent.

Now I had been on the ground for nearly a year and had gone through enough doltish base politics and drama to be jaded. So when I got word that a Special Forces team was being sent to my little corner of Afghanistan, I had a fairly good idea of how they would view a blonde-haired, blue-eyed female civilian in their territory. I was used to being scoffed at or doubted based on my appearance. More than once I got the indignant, "*You* are going out and meeting the locals?" Like water off a duck's back, I would smile politely and respond with "Someone's got to do it!"

As one of the only American civilians on the ground living in my province, I was asked to brief the incoming A-Team on my perceptions, who I knew, and what I knew.

On a blazing hot day, determined and resolute, I marched into the plyboard frame meeting room on the Special Forces' side of the airstrip in Mazar-e-Sharif, and stepped into my future. Accompanied by colleagues, I sat down. The chief warrant officer of the A-Team sat across from me, surrounded by his team of men, none of them in uniform, all of them sporting long hair and beards. Wearing black combat-scuba short-shorts and a black T-shirt, a beard and thick brown hair, the chief commanded the room.

Our eyes met and lingered for just a moment. In that moment, with just a glance, he stole my heart.

By the time I met Chief Nelson Smith, he had been in the army fifteen years, was a qualified combat scuba diver and dive master, a jump master, and was fluent in Arabic. He was the war-hardened and seasoned officer who ran the A-Team and advised the rotating captains on strategy. He had completed seven combat tours, been awarded four Bronze Star medals—including one with a Valor device—and the Purple Heart medal for his service. Nelson had become very good at what he did. He was strong, he was stalwart, he was a man among men. He deserved the room's attention, and he got mine.

I remember little about the actual conversation that hot summer afternoon. As my heart fluttered and curiosity welled within, my head screamed "Uh oh!" As a female in a war zone, women have to maintain utmost care to preserve their reputations and prevent rumors. It was impossible to be too cautious. One wrong look or casual encounter could be misconstrued by an onlooker and my reputation tarnished. The meeting proceeded, and from the outside I was calm and collected, but internally I just wanted to find out more about him.

A few weeks later, my chance came. After a long day driving on dusty, bumpy roads, the metal gates to the camp where I was living creaked as the security guards swung them open. Inside, taking up most of the courtyard, were massive American armored vehicles. My heart raced and my stomach flip-flopped. The A-Team was there, which meant Nelson was present in the compound. The A-Team had journeyed deep into remote regions to set up their camp, returning to the small base where I was for rest and refit. Later that evening, under some auspice of programming or funding projects, we sat down to talk— and we have not stopped talking.

Over the next few months, we ended up working together on reintegration and Commander's Emergency Response projects while spending time at remote bases. Our desire to be around each other grew. Nervously, like middle school students, we acknowledged our feelings for each other. Under the deep night sky and sparkling stars, our lips touched for the first time. Our first kiss could rival any best-kiss movie scene, but what was most surprising was the long embrace that followed, like our souls took a deep inhale and then exhaled, *Finally, we found each other.* Deep called to deep and my soul breathed a sigh of relief. In just a short amount of time, Nelson grew to be my soulmate and my best friend. We were romantics, idealists, drawn to the heart of the other. The next few months we devoured every moment together, leaning and then falling into love. This was the man I was going to marry.

The memories we made together in a war zone were filled with excitement and adventure, all colored by rosy glasses. We shared armored vehicle and helicopter rides, meetings, and roof-top meals with government officials. I realize how blessed I am to have witnessed my husband in action on deployment, seeing him come in from combat, smelling the sweat and dust from days on the road, watching as he led his men on night patrols, leaving the compound with helmets fitted with night vision goggles, weapons in hand.

The honor and privilege to see the man who became my husband in true "warrior mode" and to experience life downrange with him is not lost on me, as many military wives or families only experience what I did through movies or videos. I do not take this for granted.

✦

On a warm August afternoon one year later, Nelson and I held hands as we sauntered down the streets of the Old City in Jerusalem taking in the sights, sounds, and smells. After a day of touring, we ended at the Church of the Holy Sepulchre. Soberly, we climbed the stairs leading to the traditional location of Calvary. Cresting the top, we were immediately struck with a deep and profound cry of the heart. Falling to our knees, we both wept and silently prayed together. The hymn "When I Survey the Wondrous Cross" rang in our hearts: "Love so amazing, so divine, demands my soul, my life, my all."

The tenderness and holiness of the experience lingered as we made our way to the Notre Dame rooftop wine and cheese bar located across from the Old City's New Gate. Nelson had reserved the best corner table, with spanning views of the domes and spires that were lit against the evening sky. The wine and cheese arrived. As Nelson filled our glasses, I absorbed the unparalleled views. Turning back, I found him on bended knee.

"Anne, you are my love and my life. Will you marry me?" he asked nervously. I cried and laughed with a resounding, *"Yes! With all my heart, yes!"* A group of Italian monks sat at a nearby table and cheered. The fullness of joy and expectation permeated every cell of our bodies and every moment of the evening.

A few months later, deep in love and heads high in the clouds, we took our vows and two became one, blissfully unaware of how the covenant we made would challenge us to our very cores. Excited for new a beginning, I journaled:

I am so completely in love with Nelson. Thank you, Lord, for answering my prayers and pleas to bring a man into my life who shares the same desires, passion for life and love, is a true companion, and my best friend. I pray this feeling of love and joy doesn't fade with time but grows stronger as we grow together and make You core to our relationship. Most importantly, Lord, I pray that we will be a shining example to those around us on how to love, reconcile, and live according to Your will. I pray for a life of renewed love for each other, each morning. A zest for life, love, laughter, and companionship. Life too often gets stuck on the rocky shores of details, disappointments, and distractions. Help Nelson and me to stay focused on You and on each other. To continue to "let go" and not build resentment or subtle anger. Give us ears to always hear each other and eyes to always see one another for what we are saying and for what things really are.

I've been told to be careful what you pray, as God will answer it but not necessarily as you expect. I prayed Nelson and I would be examples of reconciliation; little did I know what valley of darkness lay before us in order to fulfill that prayer. We were heading toward the fire of refinement where all we knew and took comfort in would be stripped away. I was stepping into Jesus' paradoxical saying that in losing myself I would actually find myself. We were about to be recalibrated.

CHAPTER TWO

DARK DAYS

Suffering and death are not enemies, but doors leading to new lives of knowledge and love.
—Father Thomas Keating

L IKE MUSIC FADING AWAY IN the background or muffled under the water, our wedding music was still hanging in the air when my world came crashing down. Nelson got picked for an assignment that would take him on a dangerous and unprecedented mission just days after our wedding celebration. The deployment was unique and came with new stressors, as he would be separated from his full team and operating in a new arena.

Meanwhile, I started my new life in Nashville, Tennessee, the closest big city to Fort Campbell where Nelson's 5th Group was headquartered. Day-in-and-day-out life at home was very different than when we were abroad. The "fairy-tale" romance Nelson and I had in Afghanistan came face-to-face with reality as our lives merged. Everything was new: a new home, new city, new job, new family, new systems, new expectations.

The idea of a new beginning has an optimistic ring to it, but new beginnings are usually accompanied by death—death of a way of life or career, death of a self or of an identity, death of the old to make way for the new. New beginnings usually follow exposure of the ugly, the painful, the wounds long buried and forgotten, and the crumbing of the walls that kept us safe and snug. Our relationship, which started in a war zone, quickly became a war zone itself.

✧

What's Happening?!

Needing to find a job, I shifted gears from foreign affairs and pursued a teaching certification through an intense training fellowship program. I landed my first teaching job at a "no-excuse" charter school. The no-excuse charter school served Nashville's underserved, low-income, inner-city population in a prep-school environment that enforced a strict code of conduct and behavior. While the no-excuse model was heralded as a model of success in helping close the education gap between underserved Nashville neighborhoods and the wealthier neighboring counties, it was a model built on harsh disciplinary practices for both the students and teachers if they fell short of perfection. Constant criticism, threats of disciplinary action, and strict expectations governed the relationship between the administration and teachers.

Utter exhaustion sank to my core as I navigated these new waters while also navigating a long-distance marriage. One evening, a few weeks into the deployment, physically, emotionally, and mentally spent from a tough day, the phone rang. I dragged myself into the kitchen to answer it on the last ring. Nelson's voice on the other line gave me a lift and I settled into a comfy chair to chat. The conversation started casually as we caught up on the details of the day but then there was a pause.

"Did I interrupt something you were doing? Or anyone you were talking to? Seems to have taken a while to answer," Nelson commented.

"No, just working on lesson plans, responding to emails," I tiredly mumbled.

"Any interesting conversations today? Did you see my text messages earlier?"

"No and no. My phone was in my bag. I didn't pull it out all day," I responded.

"What were you doing? Where was your bag? Who were you with?"

Unhappy or unsatisfied with my responses, he now started shotgunning questions. I fumbled through, trying to answer while thinking, *Where is this coming from?* The line of questions turned into an interrogation of who I had seen, where I had been, what I was doing, and what I was thinking.

"Nelson, are you okay? What is going on?" I asked in confusion.

"I guess I am just bracing. I just don't trust other men. I am always thinking of what others are possibly thinking," he responded with a softer tone. The conversation recovered, but I was left with a deep feeling that something was wrong.

And something *was* wrong.

Within weeks, things spiraled, and he started suggesting I was carrying on with other men and entertaining their attention. "You're just kidding with me, right?" I retorted with a snort after his first hint of accusation, thinking he was playing an odd and weird joke. But he kept on pressing, and I grew angry and despondent. Too tired to engage, I hung up the phone. My head was swirling. The conversation left me in a state of shock, reeling from the accusations and complete emotional turnaround.

The intensity of teaching in a performance-based, data-driven environment acutely grated my own personal performance tendencies and now I was completely blown over by the arguments with my husband. *How did I get here?* I kept thinking to myself. *A year earlier I was in Afghanistan meeting ex-Taliban commanders and now I can barely think straight.* I felt embarrassed and ashamed.

Confusion started to cloud those early days, and I often felt like I was living in a twilight zone and would think, *Today will be different; he will be back to his normal self.*

There were still good days, with arguments occurring once or twice a week, giving two to three days to recover in between each one. But each renewed accusation or bout of jealousy was like a wave crashing on me, causing disorientation and confusion. I didn't know what was happening or what to do about it. This was not what I expected, and I had no clue how to handle the developing situation. My rose-colored glasses were slipping off my face. I journaled:

> *Major concern—something bad is happening with Nelson. Lord, I don't know what to do. Nelson and I keep fighting. He struggles with negative thoughts that permeate his imagination and then change his mood to dour, grim, jealous, overbearing, and harsh. Three times yesterday he had thoughts of me interacting with men that turned him against me. You, oh Lord, know that I am pure. This morning I awoke to accusations that I have an undisclosed email account. Inevitably the conversation, which is long distance, ends with both of us gritting our teeth out of sheer frustration and anger.*

I counted down the days until he redeployed, thinking once he was home everything would be right again, he would see and know the truth, and we could move on. I kept my head down and powered through the months of separation.

Drowning on Dry Land

Finally, the day of Nelson's return arrived. After teaching all day, I rushed home to shower, change, and head to the airport. Seeing him across the way, I waved and smiled, praying silently things would now be different. We awkwardly embraced, a palpable element of uncertainty had developed between us. Niceties were exchanged—the flight was good, the food was bad, the day was long. Then it came: "Is everything okay? Are we good? Because if it isn't, I just want you to tell me; really, I can handle the truth," his veiled question probing to hear what he feared.

Pop. My hope for a change burst. We were definitely not in a good place. What I did not realize was the initial months during his deployment were only the gathering clouds of a brewing storm.

Around the time Nelson returned, his ex-wife remarried and moved the kids to another state. The absence of his children was an acute adjustment. The fractured time he got with me between my unusually long days and overburdened workload left him unfulfilled. He grasped for safety and control. Questions, doubts, and paranoia led to ugly arguments, and what had started during his deployment snowballed. I started to term these arguments as "episodes." Within weeks of his return, episodes began to roll in like undulant waves pummeling a rocky beach.

I longed to believe the real heart of my husband could not possibly believe his own accusations. But my hopes were dashed as the complaints intensified and emotions magnified. We careened downhill. Episodes would start quietly—a few questions here and there, a missed phone call, hesitation in my responses—but with an answer he did not like or if something did not make sense, the conversation quickly turned sour. A moment of joy would quickly be quenched with a wave of negativity, suspicion, and a rising episode.

The negative thinking, the interrogations, distrust, and hypervigilance became unremitting. Soon it felt like

I could not do anything right. I was accused of laughing too much, smiling too much, making inappropriate eye contact, talking too much, talking too loudly, holding his hand, not holding his hand, being too friendly. As the criticism became consumptive, I knew less and less how to act in public.

I keep thinking we hit rock bottom but then I wake up the next day and Nelson is worse than ever. Every day he is upset, every day he is accusing me of illicit or nefarious activities or an affair. I must recount every conversation, explain why I entered any room, moved my stuff, had a particular tone, why I called or didn't call when I went to the bathroom. Every minute is recorded, every conversation dissected.

Even during the workday, at school, I was not sheltered from the storm. Going to the bathroom too many times or too close in time to the last time raised suspicion. Inconsistencies in tone and intonation, inflection or timeline led to accusations that I was hiding something or lying about my whereabouts. If I took too long to respond to a text message, my fidelity was questioned. Eventually, location, emails, and activities were monitored and scoured, looking for red flags. It was like he was managing me like he would a source, testing me for purity of narrative and intent.

Inwardly, I was depleted from running on two to three hours of sleep a night, being constantly overwhelmed by what was required of me at work, realizing my shortcomings, and then battling with my new husband at home. Fatigue ran to my bones. I could fall asleep in any location or environment. I slept through every movie. I fell asleep at wild and loud Nashville Predators hockey games. I routinely fell asleep at my computer and would wake up drooling and delirious, just to pick up where I fell off.

I am so tired of fighting with him, of feeling unknown, misunderstood, disregarded. I am purely exhausted from teaching and fighting.

Crying, yelling, I would pound my fists hard on my legs, bruising them. My body shook ever so deeply from the earthquake in my soul. Sobbing on the floor, I wanted to explode into a puddle of mush and just fade away. What could I do? I couldn't run, I couldn't leave, I couldn't reason with him; my voice was taken, my core values mistrusted. Anguish filled my soul as coldness washed over me.

The storm is unceasing. I am not handing it well and just want him to be normal. I don't know how to be "nurturing" to a man who consistently attacks me. He attacks and then wonders why I can't be loving toward him. We are not in a good place. My job is all consuming and exhausting, stressful beyond words. I am always working. There is no end to the madness.

When an episode subsided, a wake of destruction scattered around us, Nelson would plead for forgiveness and explain he only wants to trust me and feel safe with me. Once he was calm, he did not understand I was still left reeling. I would respond with anger and try to punish him with words for what he did to me. My way of retaliation was to fire zingers of harsh truth (definitely not clothed in love), disengage, and grow cold. With a hardened heart, I tucked my head down, rolled up my sleeves, and muscled though the school year.

My performance drive put me in a position to try and be the one to manage the relationship and the arguments. I found areas I thought I could control—not being defensive, not reacting to the emotion but the need, sharing with him the way he likes it, proactively pursuing him, making him feel needed or wanted. Fooled, I thought I could make it all better and eventually I'd figure out how to solve our problems.

I tried working harder, focusing more intently, practicing longer, but ultimately the waves grew stronger and the walls came crashing down. No amount of yelling, arguing, or debating convinced him; my words fell on deaf ears. Left in a pile of flesh on the floor, I was being pulled under by currents much stronger than I had ever experienced. In my journal I mourned:

"I am drowning;

Whys and Woes

Imagine a dark, stormy beach with the ruins of a fortress laid bare, boulders scattered on the sand, boulders from all the fallen parts of our collapsed marriage. The man you love is chasing you while firing an automatic machine gun. Scared, and trying desperately to seek refuge behind the fallen boulders of your hopes and dreams, you roll up into the fetal position. When the bullets cease and all gets quiet, he walks over, crying and begging you for a hug and to love him. This was what an episode was like.

Where was God in all this? I was crying out but felt like all I heard was silence and the raging storm of Nelson's episodes and this unrelenting school I was trying to please. Growing up in a conservative Christian family, I had been challenged spiritually with my own parents' divorce, and thought I was prepared for anything. Besides, I had just survived living in Afghanistan on my own. This emotional and verbal abuse, however, was far from what I signed up for, but I did not know what to do or where to turn. Trying to fix things on my own in my own strength, trying to learn to love Nelson with my own strength, I began to feel like a nonhuman. Bitterness and gall filled my inner being. "Why me, Lord?" prevailed in my journaling, my thoughts, and in my heart. The *whys* started to dominate my self-pity.

Why me? What did I do to deserve a man like this? I thought he loved the Lord and was seeking Him. But he rarely opens his Bible and doesn't actively fight his own battle. I'm at my whit's end. I am crying out for help.

Lord, why aren't you doing something?? Why aren't you transforming him and me? I can't stand this. I want to run away. I shouldn't have married Nelson. Such emotional turmoil with this walking on eggshells. Why did I marry him? But I am married. I made the choice. Now I must learn to love.

This period watered deep-seeded anger, fears, anxiety, insecurity, selfish ambition, and impatience. Part of me wanted to cling to him and beg him to get help. Part of me wanted to run away and never look back. Part of me loved him and wanted to make it right. Part of me wanted to be filled with compassion and kindness. So much suspicion, negative thoughts, accusations, and lack of trust made me emotionally reactive and defensive.

> *I'm really struggling with anger, bitterness, and jealousy. I feel so trapped, wanting this marriage to work, but every minute being careful, walking on eggshells. Anything can set him off. I get jealous when I see other's happiness. Why, Lord, why me? I can't bear this. It's too much. Such wrong accusations leveled at me. How? How did we come to this? I am so wounded and hurt.*

I allowed jealousy to pervade my thoughts, wishing I had what others had, wanting their peace and contentment. Jealousy, which is a fruit of the flesh (Galatians 5:21, Romans 1:29), an antonym of love (1 Corinthians 13:4), a symptom of pride (1 Timothy 6:4), and a catalyst for conflict (James 3:16)[2], gained traction and tread in my inner being, filling me with bitterness. With my world crumbling around me, I grew angry at God, feeling as though God had disappointed me and let me down.

> *I feel fooled. Nelson fooled me. God fooled me, and I fooled myself. I am better off alone. The feeling deep inside me is one of utter pain and torment, trapped, wanting to run away, wanting out. God, I can't continue on like this. I need an intervention.*

It was during one dark moment of the soul that the Lord spoke clearly to my heart. He said, "Be patient with him, I am working on him." Shocked, but oddly comforted, these words immediately brought hope that would carry me through the darkest days. When I wanted to throw in the towel, flee from him, file for divorce and never look back, that still, small voice would whisper, "Be patient; I am working on him."

Lord, I need you. This is such emotional abuse. I feel like a nonperson. I can't live like this. I want a divorce but I don't because I love him and I remember your words, "Be patient; I'm working on him."

I was crying out to the Lord, but where was He? Why wasn't He answering my prayers, my cries? The solution to my cries were driven by me and what I thought I could control. I was doing it in my own strength. Though I was crying out to the Lord for help, I kept my hand firmly planted on how to control. We both continued on in our own ways, backsliding further and further until we each hit our own rock bottoms.

Shamed into Silence

Transitioning to a new job field, meeting Nelson's children, navigating a new marriage, and living in a new city without friends left me isolated and alone. When I looked at my friends and compared my situation, no one else was struggling as we were, no one else could identify with how hard life was to live. I was embarrassed. Nelson and I both hail from a world of "pull yourself up by the bootstraps." Arrogance and pride kept us from reaching out for help.

I feel so much shame. I am an intelligent woman. How did I end up with a man like this? I am just so hurt, cut to the core, devastated. I have no one to turn to but God. To no friend can I tell what is happening. I am so alone and hurt that I want the Lord to take my spirit. I'd never take my own, but Lord, I'm ready to come home to You. I can't live like this for the rest of my life, day in and day out.

The need to maintain outward perception compounded by fear of what others would say if they knew the truth silenced me. I did not reach out to friends. I did not reach out to my church community. I suffered in silence and pretended everything was okay. We presented ourselves as "fine." We were engaging, entertaining, and smiled big at church. We tried to maintain the outward image of a couple that had it all together. We'd go out on the town or host parties, but inevitably, something would trigger Nelson and I'd be staring down the barrel of an episode. As soon as the car door closed, it was teeth out. "Why did you look at that man so many times? I didn't like how that man addressed you and not me," he would interrogate.

Shame shamed us into silence. No one knew of our struggles, the horrible vicious fights, and the deep sadness and anger that ran through my body.

My job takes everything out of me. Nelson takes everything out of me. No one invests in me. I have no one pouring into me, feeding me. I am angry. I hate this. I am such a negative and quick-tempered person now.

I was at a breaking point and needed to turn somewhere, to someone for help. Nearing my birthday one cold dreary day, Nelson asked, "Hey, baby, what do you want for your birthday?"

"To go to counseling," I responded cynically but truthfully.

"Why would you say that? Are you seeing someone? Do you want a divorce? Tell me the truth," he demanded in response.

"I just want help," I retorted coldly. The argument itself underpinned the very reason I wanted help.

After finding a female counselor who took our insurance, Nelson dropped me off and waited for me in the car.

I neared the office door. *What did I do to get myself here?* I wondered. Life felt surreal, like I was walking in a nightmare sequence and just needed to find the right button to change the dream. I entered the counselor's office with a deep ache in my heart that cried, *Somebody, help!*

The room had a blue hue that made me feel cold on the inside. I was nervous and anxious opening up, but at least it was to a stranger who wouldn't judge, or so I thought. I began telling our story, our fights, our arguments, our verbal and emotional wars. After the long and detail-filled session, she looked at me and said in a biting, almost sneering tone, "Why are you still with him?"

I didn't know what to say. I completely understood why she would ask that question, but it was not the question I wanted to answer. I knew deep in my soul that divorce was not an option, at least at this point. Obedience to the Lord was being patient with Nelson, but I needed expert help to obey.

After that session, I became afraid anyone I opened up to would respond in a like manner and treat Nelson like a plague or as if he had leprosy. I wanted to protect him—us—from condemnation.

Months went by. Eventually I got up the nerve to just hint at some of our issues to someone at church who seemed like a safe person. After hearing only surface tension stuff, she turned and sweetly smiling, critically asked in her southern lilt, "Well, why are you still with him? You know you can divorce him for this, right?" Like arrows to my heart, her words shut me down. I closed my clam shell tightly and kept on trying to fix the episodes, to manage Nelson, and to tread water on dry land.

My "help me, I'm drowning" flares were met with judgment and criticism and advice that I knew for me was not the answer. I knew who Nelson was at his core: he was a good man, a man who desired to always do the right thing. I did not need another voice telling me what my brain was already screaming at me—*divorce, divorce, divorce.* I needed someone to walk us through the pain and the rubble of our lives, to come alongside us, to offer us a lifeboat in the midst of the storm, to remind us of truth and help us find the right tools to use in the hardest moments.

By not being honest with ourselves and our situation, without letting others into my hurt and pain, I prevented healing from happening. Shame is from the enemy, a tool to silence us, to keep us bound by our brokenness.

We were shattered.

I feel so lost, unknown, and lonely. I don't know who I am anymore, where I should be, or what to do. My walls have crumbled and I am now a pile of rubble that Nelson keeps tripping over and getting mad at because he stubbed his toe. I am simply surviving. Surviving my marriage, my job, who I am.

Many times the desire to run away welled within me, but my heart was tethered with a thick, deep cord and the words *be patient*. My heart was screaming, *I can't be patient on my own, Lord, any longer. Help me!* I was crying out to the Lord, but I could not feel Him or see Him working.

Warmer weather and the end of the school year brought tremendous relief, like removing a tight corset and inhaling deeply. I woke up one morning to a quiet house and a broken heart, and I wept. I cried out in a loud voice, "I CAN'T DO THIS ANYMORE!"

CHAPTER THREE

CHANGING ME

Sometimes the most important thing in a whole day
is the rest we take between two deep breaths, or the
turning inwards in prayer for five short minutes.
Each of us must turn inward and destroy in himself
all that he thinks he ought to destroy in others.
—Etty Hillesum

I LAY THERE DEPLETED, THE floor soaking up my tears. Darkness and despair enveloped me. I was undone, hating my life, my husband, my situation. There in the darkness, I gave up control. There was nothing—zero, zilch—that I could do to change Nelson or my circumstances. I came to the end of myself, and at the end of myself I found Jesus. Sitting at the bottom of the pit, I looked up and there was the beautiful and kind hand of Jesus reaching in and saying, "Only I can fix this. Come to Me; I will give you rest."

As I scraped myself off the floor, I knew something unseen and intangible had shifted. The tiniest pinhole of light had pierced the darkness. Dazed and delirious, I shuffled to the kitchen, poured myself a cup of coffee, and decided to curl up on a chair to journal the previous night's episode. As my pen hit the paper, I felt a pause, like a soft hand on my shoulder, accompanied by the inner thought of *This needs to be different*. Taking a small step in the physical but a giant leap in the spiritual, I declared in big, bold letters at the top of a fresh, clean page:

July 2014: I commit the rest of these pages to forgiveness, learning to forgive, grace, and walking with the Lord on the path of healing.

School had dismissed for the summer and I found my mornings open and unscheduled, as most of my friends worked in offices and were unavailable during the day. A new routine formed: cup of coffee, comfy chair, and courage to ask the Lord for new ears, new eyes, and a new heart. More days than not, I sat weeping, pouring myself out to Him. Some mornings I just sat and stared, my heart numb from the previous night's arguments. Other days I devoured the Psalms, letting the words of David come alive in my innermost being.

And then there were the days I reasoned with the Lord, wrestling with my life's realities in light of His heart, with my heart screaming: "Hey, Jesus, don't you care? I'm doing all this work to save my marriage and it is not working! You said you came to give life abundantly, but what I'm living is far from abundant!"

In truth, I did not even know how to *be* anymore. Married but alone, treading water through a raging storm, I was either going to find my life in Christ or my own pursuits would keep drowning me. Jesus' kind response to my grumbling sounded a lot like His response to Martha in Luke 10: "Anne, come, sit at my feet, learn to *be* before doing. Let Me tell you who you are, let Me change you and rebuild you." My heart desperately needed the Savior's affirmation, wisdom, and understanding in the deep places of my soul, where I longed for the clear, pure water of Jesus.

> Lord, I seek increasing wisdom and understanding. Reunite my head and my heart, Father. Teach me to exist, Lord, not just think about being.

So I asked the Lord what I should do, how to be, how to heal, how to love. Desperately, I hoped the Lord would start by fixing my external situation, but the depths of my heart sensed I would be the first on the operating table. As a gentle and kind physician He did not overpower me all at once with all the areas that needed repair. Rather, He tenderly led me to three different proverbial pools of water to drink deeply—the pool of healing, the pool of repentance, and the pool of still water.

✦

The Pool of Healing

The first pool brought forth a lesson I had learned seven years prior but the knowledge of it remained in my head, in my thoughts, and had not traveled to my heart. After graduate school, I traveled to the Middle East to study Arabic. Soon after I arrived, I received an email from my sister-in-law about a missionary couple she suggested I meet. My first response was to recoil and think, *No way,*

I have nothing in common with missionaries. Eventually, to simply be able to check the box, I reached out to the couple.

It was a perfectly warm Middle Eastern evening when I met Jamie and Donna Winship. As I entered their apartment, music was playing, people were laughing, drinks were being poured, and a hookah bubbled on the patio that overlooked the sun setting across endless cement rooftops.

Conversation was lively and soaked in retelling of grand adventures. These people were talking about God like He was their neighbor, their best friend, and had countless stories of how God powerfully intervened in their lives and the lives of their neighbors. They relayed experiences and stories of the works of God that I thought only existed in the Bible. It was so new and disorienting to hear God referenced in such an authentic and real way, especially while people were having *fun*! I was perplexed. They were the coolest Christians I had ever met, and I wanted to know what they had that I didn't. Why did they seem to have so much freedom about them? I was thirsty, and they poured into me during my time with them, feeding me with spiritual truths I had never learned in Sunday school or from the pulpit.

Then Jamie and Donna began to mentor me, bringing me under their wings and showing me a God I did not know. They opened my eyes to the power of the Holy Spirit. Most importantly, they introduced me to inner healing prayer. At the time, inner healing was a completely foreign concept to me. True to my nature, I was skeptical at first, but soon the Holy Spirit started breaking down walls, and I longed to have what the Winships had: deep confidence in a loving and all-powerful God who actively engages with and through His creation, and who longs to heal.

Inner healing is the healing of the heart, the inner emotions that are out of alignment with the truth of Jesus, by inviting Him into the wounded places. Healing of the heart is the work of Jesus, binding the brokenhearted and setting the captives free. The process of inner healing can take many forms: from prayer counseling, Christian marriage counseling, to soaking in the presence of Christ. Inner healing is identifying things that have hurt us and then asking Jesus to free us from the effects of those hurts.

At the core, inner healing invites Jesus into the point of pain and the hurt, and allows the power of the Holy Spirit to write a new message, a message of love, acceptance, and healing. It touches our deepest suffering in the inner core of our being. Unless God heals our brokenness, we will live in bondage to our deep wounds. Like healing from surgery, inner healing is usually not instantaneous but a gradual process, as we learn to live from our true selves with right thinking.

Though I had tasted the waters of the pool, it was not until the trials and tribulations of my broken marriage did I once again approach this pool, this time drinking deeply and being changed forever. Now, seven years later, in recalling what I had learned from Jamie and Donna, I reached for my dusty but dog-eared copy of *Restoring the Christian Soul: Overcoming Barriers to Completion in Christ through Healing Prayer* by Leanne Payne. Pouring over her words of wisdom on self-acceptance, healing of memories, and listening prayer, I felt a new, resolute energy driving me to sit with Jesus. So I sat.

I asked Him to come into my heart, where the pain was overwhelming, and asked Him to heal my heart, to take the dagger out, and to hold me as I healed.

Jesus, I am undone by what my life has become. I am so hurt I do not even know how to be anymore. I have become an ugly monster to Nelson and to myself. Take back my life, Lord. Speak to my heart. Let me know I have not been abandoned or rejected by You. Hold me close while I heal. I want to be like You. Enable me to share in Your sufferings for Your sake.

Time with Jesus is like precious ointment to my spirit. Day in and day out that summer and through the first semester of the next school year, I would spend my mornings in my prayer-chair, in Scripture, learning to journal and listen to Abba, the Son, and the Spirit. Oswald Chambers in *My Utmost for His Highest* says that God's purpose is not to teach us lessons through trials, but rather His purpose through our trials is to simplify our belief until our relationship to Him is that of a child.[3] I humbly approached my Lord as a child, a child looking to their parent for affirmation, for love, for life.

Ever so slowly, I began to feel His love wash over me. Laid bare, I was an empty jar that needed to be filled with His wine, His presence. Sitting at the feet of Jesus allowed the truths I had heard, even experienced in part, to migrate down to the center of my being, my heart. It was in His presence that I started to learn what it felt like to be loved by God. It is not a fleeting feeling, but a concrete, deep knowing; it is a state of being. I was learning how to "be" again, how to feel, how to hear His voice, to listen to His truths. Only one thing I needed—the presence of Jesus. Spending hours at His feet in a time of quiet intimacy restored me in profound ways. Little by little He restored my heart, strengthened me, gave me a new perspective, and started to change the way I related to Nelson. I started to feel human again.

The Pool of Repentance

As my inner being was being restored, I prayed that Jesus would show me the areas in my life that needed to be redeemed, adjusted, and recalibrated.

> Lord, I ask largely of You—reclothe Nelson and me, give us new wedding garments. I want to put You on, receive You into my deepest self, and walk with You in obedience. If there are objects or sins that prevent this, let them be known so I can confess and be restored anew. Shine into any space in my heart and . . . teach me wisdom in the innermost place. Dress me, Lord, in Your clothes with Your Spirit so I may become the woman of God You created me to be.

It did not take long for the Lord to gently show me where I was blocking the flow of the Holy Spirit with my grumbling, my attitude, and habits of the heart. God's love for me led to conviction—not for shame or guilt—but to bring me into His enduring heart for my wholeness. It is the goodness of God that led me to the pool of repentance. Isaiah 59:1 reminds us that without repentance our own sins become a barrier between us and the Lord: "Behold, the LORD's hand is not shortened, that it cannot save; neither his ear heavy, that it cannot hear: But your iniquities have separated between you and your God, and your sins have hid his face from you, that he will not hear" (KJV).

One of the most powerful weapons at our disposal as believers is repentance. Repentance rests our souls and spirits, it brings us into right relationship with him and cleanses us from our bitterness, anger, and resentment. Repentance is telling God the truth.

There is a vivid depiction of repentance and the cleansing of our hearts in C. S. Lewis's *The Voyage of the Dawn Treader*. In the story, a cranky, self-centered boy named Eustace becomes a dragon whose scales represent the shields and walls we put on ourselves. After trying to scratch off his own scales to no avail, Aslan, the figure of Jesus in the C. S. Lewis stories, says to him, "You will have to let me undress you." Eustace's account of the undressing is particularly poignant:

> I was afraid of his claws, I can tell you, but I was pretty nearly desperate now. So I just lay flat down on my back to let him do it.
>
> The very first tear he made was so deep that I thought it had gone right into my heart. And when he began pulling the skin off, it hurt worse than anything I've ever felt. . . .

Well, he peeled the beastly stuff right off . . . and there it was lying on the grass: only ever so much thicker, and darker, and more knobbly-looking than the others had been. And there was I as smooth and soft as a peeled switch and smaller than I had been. Then he caught hold of me—I didn't like that much for I was very tender underneath now that I'd no skin on—and threw me into the water.[4]

I was Eustace, and Jesus tenderly told me that only He could remove my scales, the hardened parts of my heart. My heart was bruised, calloused, and had grown thick skin. I did not like who I was in the marriage or who I was in myself. So I asked the Lord to peel me, give me a heart of flesh, and clothe me in His garments. I petitioned for a new heart and a new mind.

Transform me, Lord. Help me see Your way and will through this pain and suffering. Restore to me the joy of Your salvation and grant me a willing spirit to sustain me. (See Psalm 51:12.)

Like Eustace, the peeling away—the exposure of my own sins and need for repentance—hurt worse than anything. But it brought life, and it brought truth to the deepest parts of my being. Repentance is the shedding of the scales, bringing me back to zero with the Lord. It was the removal of the old rags, the dirty clothes, the knobby-looking false self, and allowing Jesus to clothe me in His love and righteousness.

Staring in the pool before me I saw three main areas from which I needed to repent: a haughty spirit, self-pity, and a hardened heart.

I have a tendency to dwell on what others have done to me, to exaggerate faults and overlook virtues. I exalted myself and licked my wounds with a proud and haughty spirit. I was the victim. I had a right to feel all my feelings, to look with contempt on the man who was hurting my heart. But as I sat with the Lord, He started to reveal how my self-righteousness was not going to bring healing, peace, or joy to my life. I was convicted of haughtiness and how it kept my eyes focused on injustices, whether real or perceived, and all my husband's faults, which in turn fed my heart with a steady stream of saltwater. Proverbs 16:18 warns the reader that pride goes before destruction and a haughty spirit before a fall.

Haughtiness, or arrogance, self-centeredness, boastfulness, all attempt to rob us of God's best for our lives. We strive to accomplish more, to be better or feel better through our own self-assessment, not as God sees us. James 4:10 says, "Humble yourselves before the Lord, and he will lift you up" (NIV). I had to confess my pride before the Lord, to acknowledge that I can do nothing apart from God, and that there is no true success or breakthrough apart from the Father. I do not need to exalt myself to make me feel better. As Jesus obeyed unto death and was then exalted, when we learn to obey Him and follow His teaching, He will lift us up as we are able to handle it.

Clothe yourselves, all of you, with humility toward one another, for "God opposes the proud, but gives grace to the humble." Humble yourselves therefore under the mighty hand of God, that in due time he may exalt you. Cast all your anxieties on him, for he cares about you. (1 Peter 5:5-7, RSV)

The saltwater that sprang from arrogance fed my soul with many springs, making me bitter and resentful. As He peeled away arrogance, He brought to my attention my ever-present self-pity, which went hand in hand with haughtiness. My heart and journal were filled with whys and woes. The whys and woes were bad influences, like bad friends who only brought me down, who did not speak life into my heart and did not encourage me to look to the Cross. Whys and woes kept my eyes on myself, my suffering, my bitterness; they kept me self-centered rather than Christ-centered. Wallowing in the pit of self-pity prevented the Lord from doing His work. Oswald Chambers puts it most directly:

> What does it matter if external circumstances are hard? Why should they not be! If we give way to self-pity and indulge in the luxury of misery, we banish God's riches from our own lives and hinder others from entering into His provision. No sin is worse than self-pity, because it obliterates God and puts self-interest upon the throne.[5]

The Lord was working on my heart to tear down the walls so He could use me. I had to get out of the way so the Lord could do His thing. Rather than lament and cry "woe is me," I decided I would focus on the Lord and not myself. There were plenty of journal entries of the hard arguments, negative feelings, pleadings for help, but the tone shifted to one of "mold me, Lord."

Focusing on pain and suffering, or the grievances of one's community or tribe, leads to a cycle of vengeance and bitterness. The cycle of revenge perpetuates conflict, driving people further from peace and deepening the divide. I had witnessed this on a macro scale during my time in Afghanistan. Now I saw how the same principles were at work in me as an individual.

I was weary from focusing on my situation, wallowing in my pain and anger at my situation, allowing waves of woe to wash over me. When I turned my eyes to Jesus—to the faithfulness of the Father, to the movement of the Spirit—my heart started to turn, to see hope and a future. I repented of trying to control my situation, my pride, my anger, my shame, my hard heart.

Repentance involves recognizing where we went wrong and then telling it to the Lord, which is confession. Scripture is very clear that if we confess our sins He is faithful and just and will forgive us (see 1 John 1:9). Confession is a spiritual weapon, and a super powerful weapon at that, because as you come into agreement with the Most High, it strips the enemy of a foothold. Confession is agreeing with the Lord that my ways are not His ways, that I need Him to restore me.

Lord, I come to you for Your eyes. I want to be able to securely and confidently say, "I wouldn't change anything." Melt the remaining ice around my heart that still feels cheated, tricked, and cold. I want to be able to say, "I would not change a thing."

God is faithful, and over time (and with much heat), the ice melted around my heart and just as Psalm 40 promises, He lifted me out of the slimy pit, out of the mud and mire; He set my feet on a rock and gave me a new song in my mouth, a hymn of praise to my God. Repentance only leads to revival.

The Pool of Still Water

As my heart was softening, I was led to the third pool. I looked into this pool I saw an image that was hard to make out, for the ripples distorted it. I asked the Lord what this pool was about and quietly He stilled the ripples. The image became clear—it was the reflection of Jesus. Crying, I realized that I had never really seen Jesus, only what I thought He was like through water disturbed by my own hurts, pain, and life wounds.

From a young age, I experienced God as I experienced my parents: highly accomplished and highly critical. I experienced God as legalistic, judgmental, and hard to please. Deep down I believed that if I did the right things, said the right prayers, and performed flawlessly then I would reap my heavenly Father's approval. The most powerful and effective scheme of the enemy is to tempt us to develop wrong thinking about God. Like Eve in the Garden, the enemy makes us question God's goodness, truth, and plan for our lives. Through our own negative thinking fueled by self-pity, self-righteousness, and self-centeredness, Satan weaves a false image of God.

Matthew 15:8 says woe to those who worship Him with their mouths but whose hearts are far from Him. My whole life I thought, *Phew, glad I'm not in that bucket; this verse doesn't apply to me. I am a good Christian girl. I love Jesus.* However, my journal entries are a witness to my guilt. With my mouth I was crying out to the Lord. My mouth would say I trust Him, but my heart was clinging to control, to my ways, to my own self-interests. My heart was far from Him because it was close to me and what I wanted. Struggling on my own in my own strength, through my own pain and perceptions, was getting me nowhere; it was time to be still and to let the waters be still. I had to release control and to realign my heart—to see God for who He really is, not how I make Him to be.

Trying to understand more about the God I had known my whole life but did not really *know,* I scheduled a meeting with our pastor, Father Thomas, a genuine, caring, and deeply compassionate man. I asked him how to change how I saw God, how to quiet the ripples of my own making, to truly see Him and know Him.

"The way to transform your image of God," Father Thomas told me, "is to know Jesus at the manger, at the Cross, and at the empty tomb." He encouraged me to meet Jesus at each place, to seek Him and allow the encounter to change me. He taught me to pray: "Father, I ask You to correct and transform my image of You so I can worship You as You truly are." I started to pray this daily, to ask Him to tear down false images, to show Himself to me as Promise Keeper at the cradle, Redeemer at the Cross, and Victor at the empty tomb.

Being stripped from my comfort zones, with my scales removed, I met the most loving, gentle side of God, who tenderly picked me up and held me as I cried out for help. He stilled the waters and started to reveal His true nature to me through His Word. My hurting and broken heart, being mended by the Great Physician, learned who my Savior really is, who He is to me, and who I am to Him. He is: El-Roi, the God who sees me during the darkest days; Jehovah Rapha, my healer; Jehovah Shammah, the one who is always there with me; and Jehovah Shalom, the God of peace. God is faithful to His promises and loving toward all He has made. So loving that He sent Himself incarnated, to bring reconciliation to His rebellious child—me.

Meeting Jesus each day at one of those three places opened my heart to know Him there, His strength, His perfect love, His gentleness, His promises. God will use anything to change us, to realign us to His truths, His purposes, and His plan for your life. We are not fated to a particular life or mind-set. We have been given a way to overcome trials and tribulation and that way is through Jesus. Free will allows us the choice to ignore or resist the Lord, or to surrender and allow Him to refine us.

* * *

Be patient, I'm working on him rang in my ears often, but what He really should also have been saying is *Be patient, I am working on you, too, Anne!* Head knowledge does not have transformative power. Christian clichés or simplified Bible verses do not sooth a hurting soul. Only Jesus brings true transformation, and only if we allow Him the space in our hearts. In the presence of Christ my wounds received His balm, and chink by chink the chains that bound me were cut off.

The emotional abuse I endured daily did not end all at once. My heart did not instantly heal. The whys didn't magically disappear. The darkest of Nelson's days were actually yet before me. God's answer to my cries was not to lift me out of the crisis of the moment but to speak His word into it and over it, asking me to keep my eyes on Him. Just as the Israelites in the desert crying out to be saved from poisonous snakes hurting them, God did not take the snakes away, rather He gave them a way to be healed from the snake bites. All they had to do was look at the snake on the branch (see Numbers 21:4-8). All I had to do in the midst of my hurting heart, the storms that raged around me, was to keep my eyes firmly on Jesus. Through the shadow of the valley, yet under the protective shadow of the Almighty, I started to change from the inside out.

CHAPTER FOUR

HE IS NOT THE ENEMY

War must be, while we defend our lives against a destroyer
who would devour all; but I do not love the bright sword
for its sharpness, nor the arrow for its swiftness, nor the
warrior for his glory. I love only that which they defend.
— J. R. R. Tolkien

PREPARING TO INVADE IRAQ IN 2003, Nelson and his A-Team were tasked to infiltrate the country before President Bush had even declared war. The team's main mission was to watch key Euphrates River bridges. They were charged with calling in accurate air strikes once the invasion started and ensuring the bridges were safe to cross by the conventional Army. For days or even weeks, the A-Team had to be equipped to be alone behind enemy lines with no support.

Understanding the critical need to blend in with the locals and evade detection the men exchanged battle-dress-uniforms for local clothing, helmets for *keyffiahs*, and military vehicles for brand new Toyota Tacomas. *Wow, these things are shiny. We are going to stand out like a sore thumb*, Nelson thought as he inspected them. Removing the sheen with sanders the vehicles, their only source of protection and supply, were then retrofitted with tactical equipment and radios.

Blending well with the enemy however, had its drawbacks— they looked too much like the enemy! "Once the infantry arrived, it was hard for us to move around because they kept trying to shoot at us. During the invasion, I was more afraid of our own people. The soldiers were scared to death. They were young and taking friendly fire as well as fire from the enemy," Nelson reminisced about the wild west days of early 2003. "When driving slowly towards a US convoy we would stick our arms out the windows waving American flags, and prayed we'd be marked as friendly."

"Don't shoot! Please don't shoot me, I'm not the enemy!" rang loud in his head.

Know Your Enemy

Coming in from work I never knew which man would greet me at the door. "What have you been up to?" he questioned one Friday evening, seemingly innocently as we settled in for the night.

"Grading papers and prepping lesson plans," I respond as nonchalantly as possible while sitting at the kitchen table covered with papers.

"No really, what have you been up to?" he pushed further.

"That's all I've been doing," I promised wearily.

"No phone calls, no texts?"

"I talked to my mom, I guess, but that's it. It was a busy day with a lot going on in the classroom and two grade-level meetings," I responded, trying to derail the incoming train wreck. Inevitably, I was staring down a barrage of questions with no answer to satisfy the deeper need.

"I just want to know what you've been up to," Nelson dug deeper as the trains collided. "Why did you have two meetings today? That doesn't make sense. Is there something you need to tell me? Do you have anything to say?"

"I love you, Nelson."

"Anything else?" He kept probing.

"You are my one and only."

"That's all?"

"What do you want to hear, Nelson? Tell me so I can tell you," I responded coldly.

"I don't trust you. I think you're cheating or interested in someone," he said through gritted teeth, as my own defenses went up. "I can't rest in you, I can't feel safe with you. I feel you are constantly about to hurt me," he yelled in a rage. The dialogue spiraled as we went round and round, wounding each other and trying to get the upper hand.

As had become my custom, after every episode, whether still angry, humbled, or ashamed, I crawled into my prayer-chair and asked Jesus what was going on. *Where were You, Lord, during the raging episode? Where was Your presence?*

I waited quietly, listening for His still, small voice. There were too many raised tones and slamming doors to hear it before. Now quiet, no words came, just the images of Jesus being beaten and mocked, scorned and falsely accused. "You know my pain, don't you, Jesus? And yet you still forgave them, and you were still willing to die for them. You saw that the true enemy is not against flesh and blood." I was brought to my knees. Nelson was not my enemy; I should be fighting the unseen enemy. Nelson needed as much rescuing as me. More in fact, because I had already surrendered my life to Him on the floor months earlier.

"Lord, I recognize that I have believed that Nelson is my enemy, the bad guy, the perpetrator. This lie has caused my heart to harden, to try and protect myself, which in turn has cemented the lie in my heart. Help me. Heal me, Lord."

One Saturday morning not long after that prayer, I attended a women's coffee at my church. It was a beautiful Saturday morning, but I walked into the church feeling heavy, sad, and distracted. I worried what kind of storm would be waiting for me when I returned.

The morning was spent hearing encouraging stories of ladies who had overcome adversity in their lives. One woman in particular talked about a wayward son who gave her much strife. She recalled how she gave up control and started to fight through prayer and by anointing her home and doorways, claiming Christ's authority in her home, essentially planting the flag of King Jesus on her land and property.

I was confused and intrigued at the same time, and desperate to try anything that may help my marriage. The oil of anointing is found often in Scripture but no church I had attended ever talked about it as a tool for Christians in this present day. Following the event, the pastor offered a time of prayer and anointing at the end of the conference, and I went forward.

"I have no context for anointing, but I am going through hard times and need help," I confided quietly. The minister brought over the oil and explained, "This oil symbolizes strength, God's strength, and the fragrant balsam represents the aroma of Christ described in 2 Corinthians 2:15. The oil itself is not the source of power, God is. The oil is a marker to the seen and unseen realm of what belongs to Him."

"Will you anoint me?" I asked timidly but without reservation. Carefully I sat down, and three older prayer warriors quickly circled me, as if setting up a tent around me. I gave them a faint idea of the struggles in my life, but they seemed to read between the lines. They poured oil on my head and prayed in a way I had never heard before, binding and rebuking the darkness while releasing the power of the Holy Spirit.

"Father," the lead minister started, "you know the details of this woman's story. You are in every moment and in every space. There is a heaviness around her that is not hers to carry. A darkness that is clawing and holding on to footholds. Right now, as the cloud of witnesses, we shine the light of Christ into that darkness. In the mighty name of Jesus, we bind all tormenting spirits and all spirits of intimidation. We rebuke the heaviness and declare that the devil has no place in this child of God, no power over her; she is covered by the shed blood of Jesus. We raise the banner of Christ over her. Amen."

Like a one-two punch, the prayer was short, sweet and knocked the enemy down. They exhorted me and sent me home with a vile of anointing oil to declare the Kingdom of God in my marriage and throughout my home. I had never had oil poured on me before or bold prayers spoken over me with such authority.

Bolstered by their faith, I felt a renewed sense of purpose and strength, a new wind behind my back. I returned home surprised to find an empty house, but I immediately made use of the quiet. I pulled out the anointing oil the pastor had given me and went throughout the house marking every doorway with the oil of peace. A deep emotion started welling in me as again Ephesians 6:12 rang in my ears: "For we are not fighting against flesh-and-blood enemies, but against evil rulers and authorities of the unseen world, against mighty powers in this dark world, and against evil spirits in the heavenly places" (NLT).

I had no idea what I was doing, but I followed the lady's example from church and yelled to my unseen enemy: "No more! Not in this house! Not in my marriage!

As for me and my house, we serve the living God. Darkness is not allowed here!" I then dedicated the house to the Lord and to working toward forgiveness and wholeness. I bound the enemy in the name of Jesus using Matthew 18:18 as my guide, and I pleaded the sweet aroma of the Holy One to come and take charge of this battleground, both spiritually and in the physical space of my home.

This moment and the day I cried "I give up" were two significant markers in changing the trajectory of our marriage. These events marked major shifts in my spirit that ushered in the fighting army of the Lord, which promises to fight for our marriage.

Nelson was not my enemy. Satan is the enemy. Satan used our brokenness, our hurts, our heart issues to try to destroy us both individually as well as the covenant we made to each other and to God. I have known Ephesians 6:12 nearly my whole life, that the battle was not against flesh and blood but against the spiritual forces of darkness, but as the Lord softened my heart, the verse started to take on a new meaning and a new question started to form in my heart: "How, Lord, do I actively fight the enemy in order to win this battle?" I had not been taught much about spiritual warfare growing up, but the Lord is faithful to answer the cries of those who seek His ways, and He led me to the answers that brought strategy and victory.

Know Your Authority

The power to shut the enemy down and bind him from my house came not by me but through the power of Jesus. Growing up, my family attended a large church that had wonderful Bible teaching. I knew all the Bible stories and historical narratives of the Scriptures. However, I never knew or heard much about the Holy Spirit or the authority and power given to the followers of Jesus. My faith rested on my head knowledge of Scripture and the need to perform for a highly accomplished but highly critical God. My religion was focused on the knowledge that Jesus died on the cross so I could be saved, but it was my responsibility to try and follow the rules, live a moral life, and have it all together according to the Christian lens.

Unraveling the paradigm through which I had built my spiritual life, these godly matrons showed me my authority to wield the sword of the Spirit dipped in the blood of Christ, to stand the ground He gave me to hold for the Kingdom of God. The ground I was fighting for was my marriage and my own heart. Jesus tells me in John 14:12-13 that "whoever believes in me will do the works I have been doing, and they will do even greater things than these, because I am going to the Father. And I will do whatever you ask in my name, so that the Father may be glorified in the Son" (NIV).

"Jesus," I prayed, "take back my house, take back my marriage, take back my hardened heart, so that the Father may be glorified."

In Luke chapter nine, Jesus gives those who follow Him power and authority over all demons, and He sends them out to proclaim the Kingdom of God. All authority in heaven and on earth was given to Jesus, and He commands us to follow Him, to be His disciples, to do as He did (Matthew 28:18-19). We have been given authority through Christ to claim His Kingdom has come and to hold the ground for Him.

Satan did not have power or authority over us until he convinced Adam and Eve to lay theirs down. Jesus came and bought back our authority with His blood and resurrection, then left it for you and me to pick it back up. If we lay down our weapons, our authority, we become powerless to resist the enemy. But when we grasp the sword, wield the shield, and walk in peace, there is absolutely no comparison between the power of God and the power of the enemy. The power of God completely eclipses and overshadows any power of the enemy.

Declaring and rededicating my physical dwelling to the Lord allowed His Spirit to come into the home afresh. I opened the doors to the light of Christ to dispel the darkness. Jesus is the light of the world, in Him there is no darkness. Darkness cannot overcome light. In my own home, my territory, across my threshold, the enemy can try to enter, but I have the authority to kick him out in Jesus' name. But if we have an open door, the enemy will just walk right in.

Back in the days of single-hood when I lived with friends in Washington, DC, a real physical enemy attempted to break in. I was walking home from the metro when someone started to follow me. My inner senses said he was not a good man. I picked up my pace and ran into the front door, forgetting to lock it behind me. Out of breath, I told my roommates there was a sketchy man outside. At that very moment, he burst through the front door and started yelling and grabbing purses and computer bags. My adrenaline and anger rushed in and I ran at him, kicking him and shouting, "Get out of my house, you scum bag!" Yes, I yelled *scum bag*! It's just what came flying out of my mouth without thinking. The intruder ran off empty-handed.

The enemy is like that thief. If we leave an open door, he will come in and try and take what is not his. Open doors are things in our lives that are in opposition to God—little sins, habits, thoughts, desires that do not align with the Kingdom of God. It is our job to both shut the doors through repentance and also to get angry and kick him out of our houses when he does find a way in. We are comforted knowing when we resist the devil through Jesus he *has* to flee (see James 4:7).

In my marriage, I had plenty of open doors, as I was learning while I sat in my prayer-chair each morning. Jealousy, pride, and self-pity were wide open doors for the enemy. The enemy had set up shop, provoking anger, bitterness, resentment, hateful thoughts, and separation— stealing peace, joy, and right responses. Taking my sword, the Word of God, I fought against the enemy by declaring His Kingdom come, His will be done in my house. I relied heavily on Matthew 18:18 that says that what I bind on earth will be bound in heaven. I bound the spiritual forces that I felt were at work because of my open doors, and I asked the Father to release His spirit into our house, our marriage, and my heart.

I did not have to reach perfection or maintain a perception that our marriage was fine or that I was fine. I could pick up my sword knowing I was invited by Jesus to use the authority He gave me. Frequently, from that day on, I would declare over my house:

> I bless You, Jesus, who has conquered hell, death, and the grave. I rebuke the spirit of torment, any lying or hindering spirits that have been overwhelming Nelson and me. I rebuke helplessness and despair in the name of Jesus. Father, I ask that you loose your peace along with your power, love, and a sound mind over this household. Holy Spirit, give us a fresh revelation of Jesus in our greatest need. Amen.

Jesus has given us everything we need to overcome and defeat the enemy. Scripture tells us that Jesus has given us authority to trample on snakes and scorpions and to overcome all the power of the enemy, for He who is in us is greater than he who is in the world (see Luke 10:19 and 1 John 4:4). I had the weapons, but until now it was like I was frantically fighting a giant with my little fists while ignoring the sword in my belt. The sword of the Spirit, the words of truth, the posture of our hearts are our weapons. So I picked up my sword and started to fight for myself fight for my family, fight for my marriage.

Know Your Weapons

When an episode was in full throttle, nothing I said or did could influence Nelson's feelings or thoughts. Nothing I said or did could make him feel what I wanted him to feel. Solutions and responses were driven by me and what I wanted. The darkness that came from my anger and fretting often overtook me and clouded my vision. Turning cold and harsh, and the truths I said without love brought hurt to me and my husband.

Seething from an episode, I sat before the Lord and questioned why once again things did not seem to be working. Gently He whispered to my heart, "Pray for your husband rather than point out what he should be doing or thinking or has done wrong; your role is to support him through prayer, not direction." Reinforced in military language: wives are the air-support, providing cover against the spiritual forces of darkness as our husbands move under the direction of the Lord.

As I meditated on what it meant to support Nelson through prayer, I landed on the Lord's Prayer in Matthew 6:9-10. Jesus himself taught us to pray, "Father, . . . your kingdom come, your will be done, on earth as it is in heaven" (NIV). I stopped there. *Whose will have I been praying?* I contemplated. Convicted, honesty demanded I admit that I'd been praying *my* wants, *my* agenda, *my* will be done.

Quietly, my prayer simply became *"Your* will be done, Lord." Reciting over and over "not my will but Yours" became a conscious reminder that getting my way, my word, my last shot over the bow, was not important. Like a hand releasing a death grip, the prayer relinquished my own power and manipulation over the situation and allowed the will of the Lord to take control.

Praying His agenda for my husband took me out of the way and allowed the Spirit to do His work. Most importantly, prayer did not usurp Nelson's identity or personal authority over himself. Giving control over to Jesus was the daily dying to *my* flesh, *my* wants and will. In the midst of wanting to slam Nelson in front of the Lord and say, "Fix him, now!", the Spirit guided me to see him as the Lord does, to see the inner child crying out or to see the hurting man living from a place of woundedness.

"Okay, Lord, show me how You see Nelson. He is Your son on whom You have compassion. I pray that Your Spirit teaches him Your ways, Your safety, Your peace. I trust Your timing, Lord. Help me trust and not control."

And He responded in my heart: "Meet Nelson where he is. I see him as forgiven. I will never leave or forsake him. I have a plan for Nelson."

How I prayed for Nelson started to shift. How I prayed for our marriage changed. How I prayed for myself changed. "Father, he is Your son. Be faithful to complete the good work you started in him."

When my will came into alignment with the will of the Lord, my perspective moved from the moment of crisis to seeing the person God created, calls a son, and is chasing after like He is me. He has a plan for Nelson. My husband is not the enemy.

Paul makes it clear that the war we fight is not in the flesh, but in the unseen realm. He reminds new followers of Jesus that "though we live in the world, we do not wage war as the world does. The weapons we fight with are not the weapons of the world. On the contrary, they have divine power to demolish strongholds" (2 Corinthians 10:3-4, NIV). Learning I had authority to actively fight the enemy was a shift in how I perceived my Christian life. But fighting with authority and standing my ground was only half the battle. The other half was learning to fight in prayer. Prayer is the most powerful weapon believers possess.

Battle from a Place of Rest

During the darkest days, life was untenable. It was still all too natural to grasp for control, to white-knuckle through an episode. Trying to be one step ahead of an explosive argument kept me in a frenzy. Repeatedly I cried out to the Lord, screaming, "Help me!" Yet in the midst of my desperation, I stubbornly kept trying to fix things in my own strength and with my own wisdom. I was fighting my own battle and losing. I could not fix my husband. I tried and failed and hurt both of us in the process.

Only when I let go and let the Holy Spirit work in His gentle but strong way did things start to shift. Five months after I let go that summer day, on an unseasonably warm late autumn afternoon, I sat outside with my Bible open on my lap. Numb from another episode that had crested and fallen, I felt washed ashore, struggling to breathe. The Spirit impressed upon me, "Let Jesus fight your battles." Exodus 14:14 says, "The LORD will fight for you; you need only to be still" (NIV). Some translations say you only need to stay silent or keep calm.

It was almost unfathomable for me to grasp the meaning of this passage, as it was second nature to be defensive, to push back, to prove myself right. I had not been silent, as my angry responses to Nelson attested, or calm in my body or emotions. But the Lord gently exposed that in all my striving I was standing in the way of the Lord doing His work. I had to cease my attempts to manipulate an outcome and rather let Him do everything. I needed to "put a bubble in it" as we say to children, stay calm, and carry on in prayer, asking the Lord *how* to pray.

Around this time I heard a radio broadcast with Ann Graham Lotz speaking about how to pray. She referred to Eugene Petersen's term for praying God's Word back to Him "reverse thunder."[6] After hearing this message, God's promises became the basis for my prayers, pleading and reminding God, "You promised to heal the brokenhearted (Psalm 147:3), fight for me (Deuteronomy 20:4), give me rest (Matthew 11:28). You promise me a hope and a future (Jeremiah 29:11)!"

God's heart is protective and loving toward His children. And when we allow Him, He will roar over us and fight our battles for us. Repeated often throughout Scripture, the Lord reminds us that the battle belongs to Him! He will fight for us (see Exodus 23:20-23 and Deuteronomy 1:30). Full stop. He cares deeply enough about us to give us a way to overcome all battles with the enemy!

Hearts are hard to change, and often only through the methodical and slow massage of the Lord does the calcified heart soften. At first there were still many angry outbursts and wrong responses from me in retaliation, but with time and trial I made progress in holding my peace. Knowing my authority, praying the Lord's will be done, laying aside my fleshly desires, and asking the Lord to take charge of my situation allowed me to fight from a place of rest. And as Isaiah 55:11 declares, His will does not return without accomplishing what it intends. Prayer is the most powerful weapon we have because it allows us to rest, to be calm and yet victorious through the work of the Holy Spirit.

The truth is, since the day I cried out, "I give up, it's on you, Lord," *it* was working. The Lord was doing His work quietly and subtly, slowly repairing each of us and recalibrating our minds, hearts, and spirits one notch at a time. Hitting rock bottom and releasing control did not bring instant healing or redemption. It was a long road, a hard road, full of twisted ankles and overcoming my knee-jerk reactions. The path to healing started in my own heart and on my knees. Healing prayers started to mend residual triggers for me, bringing my heart and attitude into the right responses.

CHAPTER FIVE

STAY THE COURSE

*"When a train goes through a tunnel and it gets
dark, you don't throw away the ticket and jump
off. You sit still and trust the engineer."*
—Corrie Ten Boom

WEEKS AFTER SEPTEMBER 11, 2001, Nelson Smith was ordered to prepare for combat and soon found himself in a remote corner of the world few had even heard about months before. He had just finished the Special Forces Qualification course and was a new Green Beret. Nelson was attached to a team tasked with bringing Hamid Karzai, who later became the first elected President of Afghanistan, safely back to the country. Intense fighting arose at every turn as the Special Forces team and their Afghan counterparts pushed into Kandahar. These men were leading the charge in the south, fighting the Taliban all the way to Mullah Omar's headquarters.

Nelson had been in Afghanistan a few weeks and experienced heavy fighting and heavy losses when fresh reinforcements arrived for the final push into Kandahar. The new support guys were unproven in gun battle. Nelson, in the lead vehicle of the convoy, drove an old British-style, four-cylinder Toyota with the gear shift on the left, driving wheel on the right. The line of trucks, laden with guns, ammunition, supplies, Afghans and Americans, entered a steep mountain pass when all of a sudden the *ta-ta-ta* of bullets and machine-gun fire opened in front of them.

The lead passenger in Nelson's truck was the highest-ranking officer in the vehicle and therefore the one responsible for calling the shots. "Sir! What do you want to do now?" Nelson yelled over the *zip zip zip* of bullets. Neither response nor direction was given. Rather the commander was frantically attempting to curl into the floorboard, his feet flailing in the air, kicking the windshield wipers on and off and the gear shift into neutral. This well-trained officer had lost his composure. Over the booms of RPG and machine-gun fire, the seasoned Special Forces guy in the back seat hollered loudly, "Keep driving, keep driving!" So Nelson just kept driving, driving toward the gunfire, driving through the valley.

Keep Calm, Carry on

Combat rotation after combat rotation made Nelson grow to be really good at what he did, it became instinctual to drive toward the sound of gunfire. He was trained and bred to be a warrior, to hunt, to survive, to evade, and to use deep internal sensors to read situations and people. It takes immense courage to stay calm under fire, to control the impulse to seize up. The first *zip* of a bullet flying by often ushers in panic and many newbies start yelling frantically and become incoherent on the radio. "Calm down! Stop! Get your composure, catch your breath! Now, say it again one more time, slowly and clearly, because if I have to ask you to repeat, we are wasting time!" Nelson firmly responded as he coached fresh soldiers find their battle feet.

War is ugly. It's easy to watch war movies and think, *Oh, yeah, I'd be brave like that too,* but no one ever knows how they will react when the real thing happens and *zip zip zip* go the bullets. There is a big difference between training for battle and finding yourself in the middle of a firefight. Even the toughest men can end up yelling, freezing, and even wetting themselves.

The battle for marriage is hard. Nothing prepared me for marriage. No amount of training or dating taught me how to weather the deep waters of a turbulent relationship. I entered marriage with roses in my eyes and love songs in my ears, but when the bullets of anger and accusation zipped by, I lost all self-control and flailed about. During our darkest days I wanted desperately to run away, to throw in the towel and jump ship. Nothing I endured was what I signed up for or expected. In stark contrast to a field of wildflowers, it felt like I was Frodo walking through Mordor.

Crawling through my days and clinging to anything that could offer hope, I decided to go outside my comfort zone and attend the church's women's retreat. A few months had passed since my face-in-the-carpet moment. As providence would have it, the subject of the conference was *Fear Not; Trust in God*. I felt like a battered woman going to this conference, grasping for hope and a wind of change. Still feeling new and unknown, I took my seat at a round table toward the middle of the room.

The speaker got up, adjusted her glasses, and began. "Fear kills joy," she pronounced definitively. "Ladies, the number one most repeated exhortation in Scripture is *Do Not Fear*! Free-floating fear permeates your heart, your thoughts, your attitudes, and your outlook on life, and it prevents you from walking in the promises of our God, because His kingdom is righteousness, joy and *peace*."

My ears burned. It was like she was talking directly to me. I had so much fear floating around, consuming me, dividing my attention, stealing my joy. Now months into my own recovery, the hardest days still ushered in angst like a rolling fog: fear of episodes, fear my life wouldn't change, fear of judgment by others, fear I wouldn't know what to say or do, fear of not being known or significant. The fruit of this fear was feeling less valued, unrecognized, overly self-critical, anxious to please, confrontational, explosive toward Nelson, unsure of myself, and full of self-doubt. Days before attending the conference I had written:

> Lord, there is a raging sea inside of me. I can't control my fear, hurt, and the painful realization of the situation. The raging sea pulls me in. Lord, I need help to walk on the raging sea by not taking my eyes off You, following You. I need help, Lord. I don't know what to think or how to be. How can I say, "When sorrows like sea billows roar—it is well with my soul"?

Glued to my seat, I absorbed every word like a dry sponge under a faucet. The speaker continued, "Fear is not from God, therefore must not be allowed to remain. The spirit of fear is directly opposed to the Spirit of God, the Kingdom of God, and must be battled with the weapons of God. Psalm 34:4 reassures that when we seek the Lord, He answers us, He delivers us from *all our fears*."

Jesus will deliver me from all *my fears?* It was hard for me to imagine breathing out fear and in peace when my very core was ready to "duck and cover."

Our neighbors in Nashville had chickens. One day a hawk flew over their backyard, and while one chicken ran around squawking in fear, the other stood frozen and literally fell over dead. In fear and anxiety my emotional state was often dependent on circumstances. Like the chickens, when I sensed an episode brewing or received distressing messages, I could physically feel my pulse increase, thoughts start to swirl, and my body tense. And like the chickens, I would either freeze or start flailing around, neither option leading to a sound mind, power, or love. Fear makes us lose our minds! Fear kills!

During the conference we were charged with a time of silence and mediation. Sitting on a rock and hearing the birds singing free of fear, I asked the Spirit of God to fight for me, to free me from fear's bondage. As reasonable and sensible as my worries were, fear was contrary to what Christ wanted for me. I could justify my fear all day long, but I was choosing the enemy's strategy for me rather than Christ's.

I went before the Lord and told Him the truth: "Father, I confess my fears. I confess that I have come into agreement with these fears and allowed them to take root. In the name of Jesus, I bind the spirit of fear and release the Spirit of power, love, and a sound mind as 2 Timothy 1:7 tells me. Jesus, I give You back this territory for You to rule and reign over. Send your peace to guard my heart and my mind. I ask, plead, demand, Lord, that You give me a calm heart of peace, filled with joy and confidence. Fill me with the fruit of the Spirit—love, joy, peace, patience, self-control. Lord, hear my thunderous cry! You promise peace that surpasses understanding. I need You. Help me where I am insufficient. Grant me Your peace so that fear does not swallow me!"

Releasing thunder bolts back into heaven, I reminded God of His promises, but more importantly reminded myself of His promises. In Jesus, all fear loses a foothold. The strongman must submit to the name of Jesus and release his hold, which allows the spirit of peace to shine. Fear is a tyrant that must be dealt with or it will steal your peace. The longer fear is allowed free rein in our souls, the stronger it gets. Rebuke fear and do not come into agreement with it.

Fear does not just disappear with one prayer. It's not a one-and-done battle, rather it is a daily battle—if not a moment-to-moment one. To remind myself of truth, I wrote personalized Scripture verses on sticky notes and placed them all around the house and in my car. Especially in the immediate afterquakes of an episode when I could feel my chest getting tight, I would repeat Isaiah 41:10: *Do not fear, Anne, for I am with you. Do not be dismayed, Anne, for I am your God. I will strengthen you, Anne. I will help you and I will hold you, Anne, with my righteous right hand. Do not fear, Anne, I will help you!*

Just as Peter started to sink when he took his eyes off Jesus and focused on the storm, we, too, will be overcome when we take our eyes off Jesus and focus on the treacherous mountains around us. Choosing to pursue peace rather than fear means keeping our eyes on Jesus no matter the crashing waves, the looming mountains, or the ominous sky. Scripture tells us that Jesus is our peace, that the fruit of His presence in our lives is *peace.*

Fear is the number one factor that cripples our ability to "keep driving" through the valley. But we have the eternal promises of the Lord to lead us through the valley of death, not to stop and be paralyzed in fear together. He promises, "When you go through deep waters, I will be with you. When you go through rivers of difficulty, you will not drown. When you walk through the fire of oppression, you will not be burned up; the flames will not consume you" (Isaiah 43:2, NLT). God promises to walk us through the trials of refinement, not to leave us as sheep without a shepherd. He will always send His helper, His Spirit to counsel, to guide, and to comfort through the fire.

Oswald Chambers repeatedly admonishes his readers that it is in the valley where we are tested and approved workmen of the Lord. It is in the valley where we are turned into wine for the pouring out of others, as Christ poured out Himself for us. It is in the valley where we are refined, where our heart of stone is replaced with a heart of flesh.[7]

With one step in front of the next I hobbled through, even when I thought I could go no further. Susie Larson says in her book *Your Beautiful Purpose,* "We need painful times of refining so we will know in the depths of our being (where most lies go to hide) that our own hope is in the Living God who daily establishes his purposes for us."[8]

Check Engine Lights

The valley is full of treacherous enemies and threats. My battle between fear and peace took center stage, but there were many other deep needs to sort out. A raging sea of my emotions was pulling me down, emotions that were unfamiliar and I did not have the tools to manage. Before marriage, I had been successful at managing my own life and in keeping deep emotions and people at arm's length so I could control their perception of me.

Emotions, as I understood them, were unnecessary and too often got people in trouble rather than out of it. Stoicism had been king in my world. Like Elsa in *Frozen* sings, "Conceal, don't feel, don't let them know," my mantra was "control my emotions, hide my true feelings." Behind my mask of suppressed emotions was the deep well of a heart that needed to be touched by Abba Father and given permission to feel.

Under the pain of the situation and broken dreams, the surge of emotions broke my levees and flooded my body. I needed professional help. Wary from the first experience, I went to a counselor through a local church. "What brings you in today?" he started off, crossing his hands and legs and looking at me kindly. I explained our marriage, Nelson's combat experience, his previous marriage, and concluded, "I need tools to survive the episodes, to just survive."

My systems were overloaded, short-circuiting, and sparks were flying everywhere. So many new and unrecognized emotions coursed through me, bewildering me.

"Your emotions are a check engine light," the counselor said during one session. "They are an important gauge as to what is happening on the inside."

"But I don't know what is happening on the inside! All I know is that I am left reeling after an episode—lost, confused, and I crawl back to my prayer-chair wondering why it is so hard," I bemoaned.

"Here, take this." The counselor handed me a piece of paper with a list of words. Feeling words. "Study this list. I encourage you to find the feelings that match yours when you feel a surge or after an episode. Say them aloud; be responsible for them." I took the list entitled "Vocabulary for Feelings and Emotions" (see Appendix B for an example list). I desperately needed this. As a thirty-some-year-old woman, I was starting at the beginning with the basics, being taught like a child to recognize and name my emotions.

We don't drive a car and expect it to keep going when the check engine light is on. Emotional pain indicates we need to check our heart engine and ask what is happening. What is leading to a strong emotion or reaction? Understanding and taking responsibility for my feelings removed my logical left brain from the pedestal and gave my right-brained emotions a chance to give my pain a voice. Giving a voice to my pain separated me from the issue, taking out a feeling or behavior so it could be examined objectively. Rather than ignore my "check engine," identifying the deeper issues behind the emotions freed me to be more me, while keeping my feet on the path through the valley.

Role-playing conversations with the counselor helped reinforce concepts until they were internalized. "Nelson," I practiced sitting comfortably in my counseling chair, knowing it would not be so comfortable when I had to use this in earnest, "you are hurting me with your words. I feel hurt. I'm asking you to own how you affect me." Or when I needed to ask forgiveness, I trained, "Nelson, I care about you. I'm sorry you are hurting and in my fear and hurt I responded poorly." Each week I dragged myself to the one-hour session to be bandaged, taught, and sent back out to live what I practiced.

How I was affected in my vulnerabilities is my story. Being able to identify the accompanying feelings gave me a voice and enabled me to be the judge rather than the victim of my emotions. God did not give us emotions to squelch and ignore or on the flip side let them control us. Naming them opened my eyes to see the good and the true in myself and in Nelson and then call it forth.[9] Calling actions and situations for what they really are allows us to see through the behavior to the person God created, which in turn opens the door to compassion. Compassion was

71

recognizing the fear center in Nelson but not allowing it to control my emotions.

Nelson was going through his own battles with fear—the fear over losing his identity, his purpose, his safety, everything he had known in life up until this point. Fear of losing control. Fear of being deceived. These fears manifested in anger, bitterness, outbursts, spiraling thoughts, and grasping for control. Compassion meant not ignoring my hurt and pain to sooth Nelson's wounds, but calling his wounds for what they are, naming my own, and praying for us. When Nelson was activated, I could step back and name the deeper issue and then have compassion for him while praying against the fear. Eventually, even in the midst of the verbal onslaughts, I started to see the true heart in Nelson crying for love and safety.

Count the Costs

Out of every one hundred men, ten shouldn't even be there, eighty are just targets, nine are the real fighters, and we are lucky to have them, for they make the battle. Ah, but the one, one is a warrior, and he will bring the others back.
—Heraclitus

Baghdad, Iraq 2004. Violence and insurrection mounted daily. Nelson was in charge of running convoys to bring ammunition and supplies to different A-Team houses in the Baghdad region during the day, and at night he was kicking in doors and going on raids. Yes, he was a Green Beret, but the convoys were often driven by regular army soldiers who may have just graduated from high school. The men and women were scared. It was an intense leadership position.

Leading convoys through Baghdad and down Route Irish, once dubbed the world's most dangerous road, was a daily gamble with death. Good people were lost, millions of dollars of equipment destroyed, and deep heartache sown on Route Irish. Heavy body armor and up-armored vehicles offered only so much protection. Improvised Explosive Devices (IEDs) were placed along roads, enemy RPGs waited for convoys to slow at turns, or, due to guardrails or concrete barriers, small arms fire often riddled fuel trucks and men escaping burning trucks. Convoys were magnets for enemy engagement. But the mission must go on.

On this one day it was hotter than Hades as Nelson led his convoy through Baghdad. The convoy came to a dead stop as they found themselves in bumper-to-bumper traffic. The route was clogged and no lane was moving. Determined to keep his trucks from becoming sitting ducks, Nelson risked his life and jumped out of the lead vehicle, walking up and down the line of cars, pounding on the windows, motioning for each to move aside.

"Yataharak!" Smith yelled in Arabic through the windows. *"Yataharak, ALAN!* Move NOW!"

Inch by inch, as cars repositioned, a path opened up for the convoy.

"I walked my convoy of trucks through this downtown area of Baghdad. All my guys kept expecting me to crumble under sniper fire." After that mission, soldiers would come up to Nelson and confide to him they were scared to death of being in the convoys, but when Nelson was in the lead, they breathed a sigh of relief and felt they had a chance of making it home.

"I was focused on getting the mission done. That particular deployment I stopped worrying about dying," Nelson reflected. "In 2001, my team sergeant mentored me: 'The sooner you realize you're not going to make it out of here alive, the sooner you can focus and be a soldier.' If you think there is hope you will make it out alive, then you will be afraid to die and afraid to take risks that could save lives. To function as a soldier, as a leader, I had to think of every deployment as if it were going to be my last."

Internalizing the need to die to self does not come easily, readily, or without struggle. It is based on counting the costs. Countless explosions, hardships, and mentored moments ultimately led to Nelson's rise as a leader and warrior. Those experiences cost Nelson a lot, but ultimately enabled him to lead countless soldiers home safely.

Nelson could only accomplish the mission if he gave up his desperation to live; as believers, I learned the same lesson in marriage. Paraphrasing Luke 14:28, Jesus asks, "For which of you, desiring to [accomplish a mission, build a life together, save a marriage, heal a relationship] does not first sit down and count the cost, whether he has enough to complete it?" Counting the costs includes fiscal responsibility, but in marriage it also includes assessing aspects of ourselves we will have to sacrifice or change. When married couples fight, they are really fighting themselves; they are fighting against the price tag of the relationship; the cost of dying to self.

The first year of marriage correlated with my year of teaching at the charter school. Sleep deprived and emotionally exhausted, I was frazzled and worn thin, with little time that could be dedicated to my husband. I did not put my marriage first, I did not put Nelson first, all my time and energy went into the school, lesson preparation, and deliverables. Nelson got the remnants, the crumbs. I did not count the cost of my job on my marriage. And we suffered.

Pride and fear keep me bound to this unhealthy school. I justified staying because money was very tight, and I am not a quitter. *I can do this. I am not a quitter,* I would say to myself. But just because I *could*, did not mean I *should* have. I did not trust God enough to provide for us if I quit. It did not register in my heart that God honors the choices that honor Him, and which honor our spouses. So in my own strength I pushed through. Choosing to stay in the job sucked every ounce of energy, power, and drive from prioritizing our marriage.

Marriage should be the number one priority, not financial well-being or pride in not quitting. My pride needed to die, as well as my fears, my lack of trust, my flesh. Galatians 5:24 says that those who belong to Christ Jesus must crucify the flesh with its passions and desires. That includes pride, fear, wrong responses, and lack of trust. But we are not left dead, hanging on a cross. We are promised that when we do die to self, Christ will live in us! More than that, He will walk alongside us as we stay the course.

Crucify my flesh, so it is not me who lives but Christ through me. Subdue my flesh, my selfishness. Help me not resort to my old nature, but obey God.

Now, years later, we look very critically at all jobs and time commitments that may bring conflict into the relationship. Prayer and discernment are paramount to being successful, maintaining a team mentality, and operating in unity.

The path through the valley is anything short of a cake walk—I myself had deep issues to overcome, let alone the issues in our marriage. Yet, through it all, the Lord has shown grace, faithfulness, and a tender conviction that guides us forward.

Light at the End of the Valley

Not much of my external life had changed since I hit rock bottom eight months before. Episodes still rolled in like waves on a stormy beach. I actually had more bad days than good ones. Yet I was learning to stay the course by bringing my gaze back to Jesus. Even if my circumstances didn't change, my perspective was changing, and who I was within the situation changed.

Every fall my college friends—friends who knew me long before Nelson was in the picture—gather for a weekend reunion. The reunion that occured only five months after our wedding turned out to be a miserable experience as I tentatively balanced hurricane-force episodes with being present with friends. Incessant phone calls and interrogations tore me from dinner tables and dance floors, leading to inquisitive looks and whispers of "Is everything okay with Anne?" None of them could understand the level of inner turmoil that came with trying to balance the freedom of a weekend with friends and the realities of home life.

A thread of dread ensued as I boarded the plane for the annual trip, now my second reunion as a married woman. The "turn off your cell phones" announcement blared over the loudspeaker. I used the enforced silence to give myself a pep talk, fully aware that the tension I was about to face would feel like walking a tightrope. I longed for the normalcy of old, rooted friendships.

New Orleans was the destination city, a city with vibrant life both day and night. Between elaborate meals, long conversations, and chatty cocktail hours, the strain with Nelson intensified. The first evening went by without major incident, but I could tell he was struggling to contain a growing storm, like a weakened levee, the barriers couldn't withstand the pressure building behind them. As with every episode, something triggered a thought, a feeling, which snowballed into rage, fear, anxiety, and paranoia. Was I really where I said I was? He didn't feel safe, he didn't feel loved, he didn't feel in control. Enjoying a warm evening out, I found myself sequestered in a corner, away from the ladies while I argued with my husband.

"Hello, did your phone die?" he questioned skeptically.

"No," I responded, "we were finishing dinner and then walked to the next place. It's loud in here."

"Wait, I'm confused about your timing and our last conversation and why you aren't answering my texts. You said forty-five minutes ago you were finishing dinner," he continued.

"We finished dinner, then tried one place but it was too crowded so we moved on," I replied, exacerbated. "Can we not do this?" I said gritting my teeth while losing control of my emotions.

"I only want to be real. You're being awkward. How many places have you gone? Your tone is off. Did something happen at dinner? You don't respond to my calls and messages, and now you don't want to talk? Why not? I really don't get it. I hate this if this is a game," he pressed on coldly.

"What game?! I'm not doing this anymore," I replied just as coldly.

"I WANT A LIFE!" he yelled back.

"ME TOO! GO! Go get your life," I retaliated. And like a steaming pot under mounting pressure, the lid blew off. I lost my temper and exploded. I tore him down with my words; said things no wife should ever say.

"I can't deal with this! I can't deal with *you*! I am done," I yelled into the phone and immediately shut it off.

The phone stayed off the rest of the night and all the next day as I traveled back to Nashville. Trouble was sure to be waiting for me. All the heart healing that had started, and which only had a thin protective layer of scab covering it, was ripped wide open. Guilt and shame mingled with anger and exhaustion as I turned the key to our home.

"Hello?" I called out. But there was no response. "I'm home; I know we need to talk," I timidly tried again. "Hello?"

Silence.

He was gone.

Nelson had packed a bag and left. Now it was my turn to not be able to get in touch with him: he had turned off his phone. Weeping and hating my life, I cried out to the Lord with the same words I mumbled the day I hit rock bottom: "Lord, I can't do this anymore."

It was a long night of prayer and repentance for me. I cried myself to sleep and woke the next morning with puffy eyes and a stuffy head. The sound of my phone split the silence. It was Nelson.

"We need to talk. I'm coming home," was all he said.

An hour later he walked through the front door. I could tell something was different. He was *too* calm. I braced for him to say that it was finished, he was filing for divorce. Instead, he sat on the edge of the couch, pausing to catch his words.

"I, uh, think it's time," he mumbled, "time I turn myself in to the army psychologist."

I sat stunned. Thinking I was about to hear the words "I want a divorce," I was unprepared for "I want to get help."

"Are you sure?" I responded tentatively.

"Yes. I can't live with myself like this any longer."

Little did I know that the night before, as I cried out to the Lord for help, in a motel fifty miles away, Nelson was facing a dark night of the soul as well, crying out: "Oh, Father, please help me! I am lost. At least I feel like I am. I need You, Your love. Please heal my brokenness. No person can withstand this barrage. I know and can see what I am doing to us. I feel defenseless, a marionette puppet being manipulated by something that is not wholesome. My spirit is tired but not broken. I must do what I can to save myself for You and for my wife."

CHAPTER SIX

CHANGING HIM

Out of suffering have emerged the strongest souls;
the most massive characters are seared with scars.
—Khalil Gibran

I T WAS AN UNSEASONABLY COLD December day in 2001 in the mountains of Kandahar, Afghanistan. Nelson, a brand-new Green Beret, found himself amidst a highly trained US Special Forces team and the Afghans they supported. For three cold days and nights of intense nonstop fighting, the US and Afghan forces held the Taliban and Al-Qaeda forces at bay. The weather was so cold and the enemy so close, Nelson could feel the heat from the blast of the fire from the AC-130s as they delivered dangerously close airstrikes. But now the *ta-ta-ta* of gunfire had subsided and in its place loomed an eerie quiet.

Sleep deprived and on edge, the men focused on regrouping and reorganizing. Nelson was the communications guy, responsible for making sure comms were up and running. He was at the top of a hill chatting with another team guy when he realized the batteries to his radios were dead. Thankfully, they had just received a resupply airdrop and the supply boxes were piled in the back of Nelson's truck. He dropped his rucksack. "Hey, can you keep an eye on my bag?" he yelled over his shoulder as he jogged twenty yards down to the truck.

The sun was shining brightly as he leaned over the side and reached for a box. In an instant everything went black. Moments or minutes later, Nelson's eyes fluttered open. His head was pounding and his ears were ringing. Disoriented, he slowly came to. He was lying on his back. Kicking his legs, raising his arms, and grabbing for his weapon, Nelson quickly checked that his extremities were intact. He stood up, unsure of what had just happened. The first thing he saw were two massive holes in the truck on either side of where he had just been standing. Confused, he looked around, taking in the scene.

As his eyes began to focus, a horrific image took shape—a leg from the knee down, with boot and trousers still attached, bloody at one end, was laying on the ground next to him *That's weird. What is that? Wait a minute, that's a leg, just a leg.* His mind raced, trying to make sense of what he was seeing. "Imagine just standing there and— *boom!*—the next moment there's a leg. My mind couldn't process what I was seeing at first," he recalled. Then the little pieces started coming together and his brain realized something tragic had happened.

"First time you see such carnage it is surreal, so much death everywhere your brain can't figure out what it's all about. Your brain doesn't have the ability to figure out what it is witnessing. It's like a scene in a movie," Nelson reflected with a thousand-mile stare.

Dazed and confused, he started to look around to see what was going on. Dust and smoke clouded his view. A teammate came running toward him, blood covering his face. "Incoming!" he yelled. The two ran to the opposite end of the hill and jumped into an old Soviet fighting position. Thinking it was incoming Taliban artillery, they started scanning the ridgeline of the mountains and the riverbed, looking for the attackers. All seemed too quiet, and they wondered where everyone was.

Just then another guy came running and fell into the hole with them. Though he couldn't see the blood at first, Nelson could tell his teammate was in a lot of pain. He was holding half of an AK-47. "I can't feel my legs," he kept crying. "Something is in my back!" Nelson pulled the guy's shirt up and saw a nickel-sized hole in the man's back, blood slowly draining from it. Risking exposure, the two of them decided to leave the fighting position to get their friend to the medic.

Supporting the wounded teammate between them, they walked down the hill. The smoke was clearing and the extent of the carnage started to become apparent. All the vehicles were smoking, tires flat, windows gone, and the sharp smell of diesel fuel permeated the air. Nelson looked down and saw a totally intact groin lying on the dusty ground.

As they approached the command post he could see three or four more people bringing in casualties. The medic was leaning against a wall with blood streaming down his face. Someone yelled, "This is the casualty collection point. Bring all wounded here!" They handed their wounded companion to the medic and turned to help others.

By now, people were screaming everywhere, screaming for help. Calm under pressure, Nelson immediately started separating the wounded from the dead. Bodies seemed to be everywhere. He came to one body lying face down in the dust, blood all around. He turned him over and saw the face was totally gone; just a black hole remained. Internally, Nelson thought, *Okay, he's dead. Check the next one*, and then he moved on to the next body.

"We picked up bodies, parts of bodies, missing heads, pieces everywhere. Too many to count. We stacked the dead against the wall, pieces and parts. Rows and rows." He saw a group of men carrying a body in a blanket. As they passed him, he saw a charred body with no head, just shoulders down, "like a burnt end of a cigar." The blast had killed people hundreds of yards away.

The collection point was filling quickly with the wounded and dead. "Smith, come here, I need your help!" a teammate called as he bent over another body. Nelson was instructed to hold the back of the head while the other guy got more bandages. As they switched hands holding the head, the back of the man's head fell off with part of his skull. "I could see his brain," Nelson recalled. "I could see the gray matter pulsing with the man's heartbeat." Quickly he pushed the bandage and everything back in. The man held his hand out for Nelson to hold it. "He was wearing a black glove but the middle of his palm was blown out. I could see right through it, tendons and bones.

I could see right to the ground." Nelson stayed with him until more bandages and help arrived, then turned his attention to getting communications up and running.

Remembering his rucksack and radio at the top of the hill, Nelson started back to get it but stopped short as he looked down and saw another teammate, his body ripped in half, his beard covered in dust and specks. "Help me," he gasped to Nelson as he raised an arm toward him. Nelson stopped and kneeled beside him as his comrade blankly stared at the sky, gasping for breath, entrails and guts spilling onto the sand. Unable to do anything to help, Nelson took the man's hand and held it tightly as he took his last breath.

Hoping to find his comrade whom he had been with before the blast, Nelson continued on and crested the hill. He came face-to-face with a stack of bodies piled from the blast. Their clothes and shirts were blown off. "I couldn't tell where one body ended and the other began. It was just a big pile of meat," he recalled soberly.

Nelson spotted his rucksack next to the bodies. He needed to push some of them out of the way to reach it, but he did not spot his teammate. He did, however, notice another American teammate on the other side of the stack of bodies. The man was barely alive, his eyes rolled to the back of his head, vomit, and wet pants caked his uniform. Nelson dropped the rucksack and yelled for help. Within seconds someone arrived. They grabbed the teammate's head and legs, but as they lifted him up, RPGs started exploding around them. They were thrown sideways, dropping their friend. Feelings of shame and sadness coursed through Nelson as they picked the soldier back up and got him to the collection point. Unfortunately, the shrapnel in the teammate's brain ultimately took his life.

After many hours, a rescue was launched to help the beleaguered team. A wearied Nelson began the arduous task of handing dead and wounded comrades to a flight surgeon to be medically evacuated. Realizing he still had not seen his buddy, Nelson went searching for him. For hours he sifted through debris, looking for a sign of the missing man. About ready to give up, Nelson spotted something under a pile of rocks—the baseball cap that his friend had been wearing. Nelson slowly reached down and gently picked it up. Inside was a chunk of flesh—all that remained of his friend. The very spot where Nelson and his mate had been chatting received direct impact of the bomb. Men one hundred yards away were decapitated. Nelson, twenty yards from ground zero, survived.

"You can't push pause," he said. "It was tough, but we had to carry on. There was no time-out. We reconsolidated, got reinforcements, continued on, and ultimately the Taliban surrendered a couple of days later."

December 5, 2001, will forever be lodged in Nelson's being as the hardest day of his life. As time would tell, the horrors of the day were a result of an errant friendly bomb. Following the battery change on a faulty laser-guided system, the coordinates for the bomb drop reset to the A-Team's position and a 2,000-pound Joint Direct Attack Munition (JDAM) bomb, the size of a car, landed on Nelson and his team and the friendly Afghan forces.

* * *

Ten months of our first year of marriage Nelson was deployed, training, or away at school. Our long-distance marriage was stressed beyond comprehension, and we limped to our first-year milestone, torn and tattered. To celebrate our first anniversary, I flew to Fort Bragg (now named Fort Liberty) where Nelson was attending a three-month course. I arrived exhausted and drained, but still wanting to make the most of seeing my husband.

We celebrated by heading to Wilmington Beach, where we dined on oysters and martinis at a beach-side tiki hut. Finishing our meal, we got up to see the sunset. The unfettered breeze, undulating waves of the ocean, and the warm sand all seemed to quell the episodes, and for the first time in a long time I felt connected to my husband. We sat together, no words spoken, just feet buried in the sand. Something deep in my chest loosened and uncontrollable big, hot tears poured down my face. My husband, whose vitriolic words had cut me to the core for months upon end, wrapped his arms around me and in a moment of deep calling to deep, his pure God-formed image dominated his broken, hardened heart, and we were reunited. It was a tender moment, a moment when our spirits were reminded of what drew our hearts together in Afghanistan.

The next day we lounged on the beach, and as the sun lowered in the sky, we readied to leave. Unexpectedly, Nelson jumped up and headed toward a man walking on the beach with his dog. The man was wearing a tan khaki hat with the Special Forces regimental crest on the front. Nelson introduced himself to the man and they started talking. I hung back, not wanting to trigger an episode or be nosey. Eventually Nelson waved me over. As it happened, the man had been the flight surgeon on the helicopter evacuating the wounded and dead from the site of the bomb in 2001. My jaw dropped. Of all the people to randomly run into, it was someone who had been there during one of the most gruesome and impactful days of Nelson's life.

The two men talked about December 5th, both agreeing it was one of the most horrific battle scenes they had ever seen. Then, out of nowhere, the man started telling his own story of post trauma and depression. His advice to Nelson: get help before you get out because your world will come crumbling down. A man Nelson could respect through a shared experience offered words of truth that pierced the tiniest whole in Nelson's armor that, and with time and tears, allowed the thought to be seeded: *Maybe I should get help.*

A Father's Insight

More than six months passed between that providential encounter on the beach and the explosive fight during my girls' weekend before the seed sprouted. We sat quietly together, absorbing the fruit of those seeds in his declaration: "It is time for me to see the army psychologist." Hesitantly I asked if he would be willing to meet with Father Thomas before scheduling his appointment. He agreed, and I emailed Father Thomas, requesting an emergency meeting. Thankfully, Thomas had availability that very afternoon.

We awkwardly sat on the couch in Thomas's cozy office lined with books upon books and unique tokens from his travels. In his normal, nonchalant way, he asked, "So what's up?" Our troubles spilled forth: my lack of sleep, my horrible teaching job, Nelson's tendencies and outbursts, his pervasive fear of losing control, our nonstop fighting, the "night clearings." (On a regular basis, I would be jolted awake by Nelson leaping out of bed. He would wake up thinking he had heard something or seen a shadow and then would proceed to "clear" the house to make sure no intruders were present. He would go room by room, closet by closet, with his loaded gun, ready to take on the unseen enemy. Some nights Nelson was convinced he had seen a shadow and would wait in stillness, listening for any unfamiliar sound, then go clear the house. No amount of reassurance would convince Nelson that his mind was playing tricks on him. Sleep eluded him nights on end as his hypervigilance took control.)

In response to the night clearings, Thomas asked Nelson, "Do you think this is normal behavior?"

"Yes," responded Nelson, "isn't it? Doesn't every man think about the security of his home?"

"Yes, they do," Thomas affirmed, "but not by clearing their house every night with a loaded gun."

Nelson quietly absorbed this data. Sometimes information can only be heard under the right circumstances or by the right bearer. Nelson truly thought he was keeping me safe so no amount of my reasoning could assuage him. Father Thomas sat back, crossed his legs, and exhaled. "So, Nelson, you are experiencing hypervigilance, irritability, angry outbursts, not sleeping, repetitive distressing thoughts?"

"Yes," replied Nelson.

"Sounds like Post Traumatic Stress Disorder to me. These are all symptoms of PTSD," Thomas calmly synthesized.

The room fell silent. *What? PTSD? No way. Green Berets don't get PTSD.* We shifted uncomfortably, trying to digest this information. Thomas tried to help us see that deep heart wounds from Nelson's previous marriage compounded with nonstop combat deployments and witnessing death, destruction, and devastation can leave anyone vulnerable to disordered stress.

Exes and Ohs

When Nelson proposed and I tearfully and truthfully responded, "Yes! With all my heart, yes!" to the question young girls dream about being asked, I did not know what I was saying yes to other than I knew our hearts beat in rhythm and the song of our hearts was for each other. The *yes*, as so many loved ones and spouses learn, is the shortest word with the biggest impact. With it came yes to his past, present, and future, and vice versa. For both partners in a marriage or committed relationship, the past does not disappear with the newness of the relationship.

The past, which paved the way for the relationship in the first place, has a way of trying to dictate the course of the future.

Nelson comes from humble beginnings, the son of an enlisted army sergeant and hardworking mother, both of whom hail from a small town in far southwest Virginia, deep in the Appalachian Mountains. Nelson graduated high school and with little direction, decided to join the military. "My father was in the military, but that wasn't what prompted me to join. I was like a leaf blowing in the wind, not really knowing what to do with my life," he said. "I didn't know what else to do, so right after I graduated high school I joined the army."

Following boot camp, Nelson was sent to Fort Gordon to train as a radio repairman. A hot summer night outside the gates of Fort Gordon changed his life forever. Nelson met and then married his first wife, and his first daughter was born a few months later. He was young and describes his naivete as "not being able to find his bottom with both hands." At twenty years old, Nelson got married and had his first child.

What started in the heat of a summer night, cooled under the intensity of mounting secrets, extreme emotional swings, self-destructive behaviors, and fiery "midnight arguments." Nelson describes his first marriage as a "casualty of war," both the physical war he fought abroad and the wars he battled on the home front.

Naturally there were good times, and times of joy welcoming two more children. But love turned sour, and the good times were increasingly overshadowed by arguments, manipulation, guilt-tripping, and poor choices. The inherently chaotic and unstable relationship left a traumatic imprint on him. "It was toxic and overwhelming, and I felt completely out of control," Nelson reminisced to Father Thomas that day on the couch.

"Nelson, Nelson," Father Thomas compassionately interjected, "trauma does not just set in from combat, major accidents, and death. All those are big *t* traumas. What you are experiencing is both big *t* and little *t* trauma. Little *t* trauma is repeated trauma like being bullied, not experiencing love and belonging in childhood, a difficult work environment, relational issues, and such."

Nelson was experiencing PTSD from a long-term tumultuous marriage that had been imbued with manipulation and gaslighting. And like Chinese water torture, each individual drip may not hurt at the beginning, but persistent dripping causes great agony and pain. His distrust of people, hypervigilance, dislike of crowded spaces, angry outbursts, and retreating into late-night house clearings came from combat. The extreme jealousy, always looking for the negative angle, seeing the opposite sex as inherently dangerous came from the battle at home.

Pushing back tears, shoulders shaking, Nelson thought a bit and then added, "I have internalized so much pain, in a way it's like I've taken on my ex's mantle and become her. I don't know what to do or how to change."

Hearing the term PTSD caught our attention, and for the first time we both realized something deeper was at work, something that could not be willed away on its own. However, the stigma against PTSD and mental help in the Special Forces is real and rooted. As a Special Forces operator, claiming PTSD amounted to humiliation and rejection, which underscores the strength it took for Nelson to seek help. Not allowing the hit on his pride to keep him trapped, Nelson pursued one of the hardest paths in his career—taking the steps for healing the inner wounds that impacted his external life.

Process the Pain

We were forewarned this day would come even before the beach encounter, before we were even married. During a premarital counseling session, the counselor probed us with questions about how we respond to life's uncertainties, major life moments and things that shape who we are as individuals. As we ended the session, the counselor paused and looked at Nelson. "You have a lot to process, Nelson. You can't process all the trauma and experiences of combat in the middle of living in the action or your brain may shut down. But your brain stores these memories away to be dealt with when it can focus on healing. There will be a day when you step off an A-Team that you will confront all you have seen and done and what has been done to you." That time came sooner than expected.

With seven combat deployments, the death of friends and teammates, being blown up and ambushed, and battling home life, Nelson could not stop and process all he had been through until he transitioned away from the intensity. Divorce and nearing retirement slowed Nelson's gait just enough for his levies to break. The intimate knowledge of the smell of burning flesh, the horrid sounds of the dying, the remnants of combat and prolonged years of war become a part of these men's souls. If we don't heal our past, we continue to walk in it. Our trauma can consume us if we let it. The pain felt is real and hurts, but at the core, pain is an indicator light that something isn't right.

Once trauma takes root, it generally takes professional help to overcome,[10] though there can be a delayed reaction in PTSD symptoms years later when something triggers it.[11] For Nelson, his triggers were the divorce and his kids moving away, a new marriage, and transitions that came with an end of a career. PTSD makes life unmanageable for both the one suffering and their loved ones. Renowned psychologist Dr. Francine Shapiro describes the effects of PTSD: "It pushes people into trying to do something to survive the chaos within them."[12] Strong emotions and responses again serve as the check engine light to stop and seek help.

Nelson, this hard-as-woodpecker-lips seasoned warrior, humbly approached the army psychologist on base for help, and after a month or two of counseling he was referred to Dr. E. C. Hurley at the Soldier Center in Clarksville, Tennessee. Dr. Hurley specialized in treating military personnel and veterans suffering with complex PTSD issues. Dr. Hurley was a godsend. To make the fit even better between doctor and patient, Dr. Hurley was from the Appalachian area like Nelson and could relate to his upbringing and family background. This was a man Nelson could respect and "hear." And he was a believer.

Dr. Hurley was also a leader in EMDR therapy. EMDR stands for Eye Movement Desensitization and Reprocessing, a method that helps the brain integrate traumatic memories and emotions. Dr. Francine Shapiro developed the method and explains in her book *Getting Past Your Past* that unprocessed memories are "stored in the brain in a way that still holds the emotions, physical sensations, and beliefs that were experienced earlier in life."[13] When the memories are triggered, the person re-experiences the emotions and sensations from the original memory, which can cause the symptoms of PTSD.[14] Though EMDR is relatively new in the field of psychology, the method has shown strong outcomes for combat veterans processing physical and emotional injury.[15]

When trauma goes unprocessed or is not adequately processed, the survivor can remain in a state of alert even when there is no immediate danger. Deep in the brain is the amygdala, the center responsible for detecting fear and preparing the body for an emergency response. Dr. Bessel van der Kolk, in his book *The Body Keeps the Score,* calls this the brain's "smoke detector." Perceived threats trigger alarms deep in the amygdala, which lead to fight or flight responses. There were perceived threats all around us and we seemed to live in a perpetual state of fight or flight. Any little thing could set Nelson off. In my journal, I recorded:

Nelson's thoughts remain bizarre, broken, accusatory, and overwhelming. He fabricates the most negative assumptions and questions me religiously, not believing me unless he hears what he wants. And yet he complains I don't love him; I don't show him love. What I do show him he says is not genuine. He's insistent and can't calm himself down.

He couldn't hear me, he couldn't calm himself down—his amygdala was hijacked. Not being able to reach me, crowded spaces, perceived inconsistencies were all triggers for Nelson, and he would leap into an activated state. A rush of emotion would flood his brain and body as his subconscious memories with all their associated emotions, sensations, and beliefs seized his responses.

EMDR therapy changes the way a traumatic or harmful memory is stored in the brain, reprocessing the attached emotions and beliefs and thereby removing the "sting" of the memory and the symptoms it produces in the present. The reprocessing comes by stimulating left and right brain conversations through back-and-forth lights or sounds, processing the triggered emotions in the safety of the counselor's office. The original memory is accessed, brain connections changed, and then the memory is stored in new ways.[16] Dr. Shapiro says, "As a result of EMDR processing, internal connections can be made rapidly during the session, as indicated by positive changes in emotions, insights, new memories, and a greater understanding of life issues."[17]

When Nelson started processing the memory of the December 5th bomb and watching his friend die, he described the memory in detail while also talking about how he felt at the moment. He felt powerless, that he couldn't help his dying friends, and felt an acute lack of control. This was a root memory, and by reprocessing the emotions associated with it, the ripple effect was far-reaching.

Under the careful and compassionate hand of Dr. Hurley, Nelson started to reprocess memories from combat wounds and memories from previous marriage wounds. Session after session, Nelson bravely brought his subconscious forward in order to be reworked and healed, and little by little the ground under him grew more firm, memories were processed.

Through regular counseling, both individually and together—including many emergency sessions and the powerful tool of EMDR—we made significant progress on the path to healing. The importance of counseling in bringing restoration cannot be understated. The freedom and safety we found being able to share the ugliest of uglies with a nonpartisan party was life-giving.

In the early days, we were in Dr. Hurley's office once or twice a week. Nelson would go through EMDR one day and then the next we went to marriage counseling. Our under-construction site sign grew bigger during these months. We were clearing old rubble and debris and trying to build a new house that would last. It was grueling work. Marriage is always hard work, but we were each healing heart wounds and building trust in each other. It would take years of dedicated rewiring of the brain to train us how to think and how to rightly react to emotions and stimuli.

One day, sitting on Dr. Hurley's sofa, he turned to me and said, "When Nelson is on solid ground, it is highly likely you will then need EMDR to process your own triggers from the last few years." And I did. I found that after Nelson was more stable, I was still responding with knee-jerk reactions and being far too defensive. When an emotion is bigger than the response requires, something is out of sync. So I too took hold of the paddles and watched the lights as I processed some of the hardest memories since being married. Hurt, anger, helplessness, and resentment were overwhelming feelings that I processed. With time, when Nelson asked where I'd been, I did not shut down, bracing for an episode, but could engage with level emotion and a clear mind.

After successful treatment with EMDR therapy, "affective distress is relieved, negative beliefs are reformulated, and physiological arousal is reduced."[18] New associations are forged between the memory and present-day responses. EMDR is a beautiful therapy, and I feel like it so richly aligns with inner healing. Scripture makes it extremely clear that to be able to discern the will of God we must renew our minds and be transformed (Romans 12:2). Saint Paul understood that for us to operate in the fullest capacity that God created us to be and to be able to know His will, we have to undergo both physical and spiritual EMDR.

When the sun started to set on Nelson's fighting days, he hung up his sword and shield and removed his armor. Standing in the mirror was a tired man who longed for the deep embrace of the Healer, the One who held Nelson's heart in His hand through each battle, the One whose angels had thrown their arms around Nelson, shielding him from blast after blast. It was at this junction in his life that the tsunami wave carrying all he had witnessed, been a part of, done himself, came crashing down on the ramparts of life. The storm brought destruction, but it also brought new opportunities and cleansing water. The old had to go to make room for the new. Zechariah 1:16 brings promises of restoration: "I will return to Jerusalem with mercy, and there my house will be rebuilt" (NIV).

May the Lord bring restoration to my soul, restoration to Nelson's mind, heart, soul. Lord, return to us and rebuild Your home in our hearts.

CHAPTER SEVEN

CHANGING US

*To be yourself in a world that is constantly trying to make
you something else is the greatest accomplishment.*
—Ralph Waldo Emerson

*Your real, new self (which is Christ's and also yours, and
yours just because it is His) will not come as long as you are
looking for it. It will come when you are looking at Him.*
—C. S. Lewis

OUR MARRIAGE WAS STILL DEEPLY fraught with division, anger, and sadness. Despite the progress of counseling and EMDR, we were very much at each other's throats. The path of reconciliation is long—and for the long-suffering. The weight of marriage exposed a multitude of weaknesses in the walls both Nelson and I had constructed throughout our lives, and the shifting sands on which they were built. With our walls in rubble, we were confronted with figuring out who we were as a couple and individually. The process of healing started with taking a long, hard look in the mirror and coming face-to-face with the influences that shaped our hearts, minds, will, and ultimately our identities.

But who was I? Who was Nelson? What exactly *is* identity? Was identity the sum of our interests, talents, and passions? Is it our job, our roles, our positions? Is identity rooted in skin color, our cultural norms, education, tribe, team? Can identity be challenged when everything is taken away, humiliation abounds, and despair takes root? To many, including myself, the answer was yes to all the above. To survive the trials and challenges of our lives, we build walls and false identities to secure ourselves, to feel safe and in control.

Making the Cut

On a frigid February day in 1999, Nelson arrived at the Special Forces Assessment and Selection, called "Selection" for short. The first step to qualifying as a Green Beret is passing Selection, a three-week test that pushes aspiring soldiers to their mental and physical limits. The test is designed to make candidates' cortisol skyrocket in an intense process to filter out the weaker ones. Upon check-in, candidates were stripped of their identity by being assigned a number. For three weeks, Nelson was just "number 163."

"Going in, I knew very little. I knew it would be hard and I would have to carry things. And I had heard a bit about Team Week," Nelson recollected with a smile.

More than three hundred candidates started that February. The first two weeks tested their individual resolve and fortitude through events like land navigation, strength testing, and ruck marching. Ruck marches were regularly 12 to 24 miles carrying a 70-pound sack through thickets, swamps, and icy marshes up to the chest. "They never tell you how far or how long, just, start rucking. When tired, I just pushed harder. I never knew what was coming next," Nelson recalled when describing those long days and nights. "All I knew was every day that went by the line got shorter and shorter in the chow hall for food. The first week we lost about a quarter of the class, the second week about 50 percent of the class. Then came Team Week."

Team Week is the hardest week of the selection process. Candidates must operate together to accomplish grueling tasks impossible without ingenuity, problem-solving, and teamwork. Yet successfully completing Team Week automatically meant selection to move on to the next steps in being awarded a Green Beret. Various factors like the psychological test, personality, or just not seeming like a good fit on a team can lead a candidate to being disqualified or asked to repeat Selection.

This Selection Day only forty of the men had made it through to the end. One cadre came forward and called a dozen names and led those men to a nearby tent. Another cadre called another dozen names and led those men behind the chow hall. Cheering, hooping, and hollering resounded from the tent. Silence came from the chow hall. Nelson and the remaining men nervously remained standing with bated breath.

A third cadre came forward. "This is the toughest part of my job," he said. "Not many men make it this far, so no matter what I say to you, keep your head held high. I regret to inform you that you will all continue on the Special Forces Qualifying course. Congratulations! It only gets harder!"

A rush of emotion, a swell of adrenaline coursed through Nelson's body. He had made it; he was selected to continue on. "I was standing among these seasoned warriors—and I had made it. It made me feel like I belonged. I kept that same mentality throughout the qualifying course. I was so proud to now be part of that; it gave me confidence that I had earned it."

Following the intensely stressful three-week selection process, candidates then enter a 53-week qualifying course that included mock invasions, interrogations, and Survive Escape Resist Evade (SERE) training, while also training for a specialized job field. The Q-course is longer and tougher than Selection and refines these men to be the tip of the spear in unconventional warfare.

Nelson's identity as a team-guy hardened through war. First in Afghanistan in 2001 and then in Iraq in 2003, he was forged as a man through the sands of war. For fifteen of Nelson's twenty-year career in the army, he served as a Special Forces Operator, earning numerous awards, military distinctions, and accolades. He was a leader among leaders and a warrior among warriors, but his identity was built on being in Special Forces.

Balancing the stress of combat on the battlefield and at home, Nelson found safety and comfort in the steadiness in his A-Team brotherhood and with his three kids. Nelson found solace in his men and felt most secure when he was in combat doing what he was trained to do. Shared laughter and the pure love and joy of his children brought a sense of safety and well-being while home. Through the hardest nights of battle, the love and desire to be with his kids kept him fighting. However, as beautiful a blessing as children are, when they become a refuge and source of emotional security, the waves of change can leave destruction on the heart. After his ex-wife remarried and the children moved away, the loss of proximity and intimacy cut Nelson to the core.

To compound all that was transpiring early in our marriage, tragedy hit the A-Team in early summer 2014 while deployed back in Afghanistan. During a fire-fight with the Taliban, a friendly fire bomb killed two of his men. Unable to deploy with his men due to attending a three-month course at Fort Bragg, Nelson was left grappling with the deaths state-side. Fresh off encountering the flight surgeon on the beach, memories of the 2001 bomb flooded his mind and heart. Survivor's guilt took over as he thought that if he had been there as the Warrant, he may have been able to prevent their deaths.

Later that summer we attended his teammates' burials in Arlington, both on the same day. It was a heart-wrenching day, witnessing the cries of the spouses and fatherless children. The A-Team, hardened Green Berets, mourned their brothers and grappled with their loss. Following the funerals, drinks were poured, memories shared, laughs and tears rolled across the Arlington,

Virginia, bar as is Special Forces' tradition of celebrating a fallen hero's life.

This awful incident was another gut punch to Nelson as feelings of inadequacy and lack of control swirled around him, leaving him grasping for answers. The waters in his soul surged as the storm raged inside. When Nelson hit his own rock bottom, months after the tragedy, he decided it was time to leave the demands of an A-Team, prepare for retirement, and focus on his healing journey. The wrenching away brought unexpected struggles, compounded with processing years of pain residue. Without his support network—his brotherhood, what was familiar to him—he was lost.

The Three Ps

Throughout my life I, too, had built a number of internal structures whose foundations were built on self-preservation, navigating family issues, social pressures, and faith. I grew up in a typical suburban Christian family, attending Christian school, going to church every Sunday, and weighing all decisions through the lens of right and wrong. I was protected in a comfortable bubble from the real world.

Both my parents were highly educated and highly critical. Academic success was the key to success, and competition was an emotion in my family. In a large family, having my voice heard was a matter of having the most clever or interesting thing to say. My identity was forged, in part, by having the right argument, winning the argument, and being intellectually competent. Winning amounted to perfection; performance and perfection were tightly integrated in how I saw myself and others, and if in doubt, look the part for perceived perfection. Thick, fortified walls of perfectionism, performance, and perception enclosed me, providing security and control.

These walls served me well for decades, encouraging me to push myself to always be stronger, smarter, more advanced. From the confines of my walls, I made friends easily, debated my way through higher education, proved my determination and abilities through travel, adventure, and then the challenge of taking the job in Afghanistan. Like Eve, I, too, had found my identity apart from my Creator and believed the lie that I could be self-sufficient. I was blind to the many ways I entered marriage from this place of brokenness and misplaced identity.

Storms of life have a way of revealing the truth and exposing lies. As expectations of a romanticized marriage unraveled, I also underwent an identity crisis becoming a teacher. During the transition to teaching, I realized just how much stock I had placed in my previous roles and jobs. My proximity to world events and unique experiences often afforded me the most interesting stories at a dinner table. And I loved it. I loved feeling set apart. But I hadn't realized how much of my identity had gotten wrapped up in it. Now I was "just a teacher." I came face-to-face with my own false identity and my pride. Under the weight of a struggling marriage and crushing job, the three Ps on which my identity rested, buckled and collapsed. I was left bare and exposed.

Living in the nightmare of my marriage, the paradigm through which I had seen the world and relationships was shattered. My identity, the ramparts of perfectionism, performance, and perception—buttressed by a deep need for acceptance and fear of rejection—had collapsed.

Clearing the Lies

Something Donna and Jamie (my mentors while I was in the Middle East) told me years before came ringing in my ears: your perception of yourself is not always the truth, and the truth about your identity is not always your perception. Our walls eventually define us and who we are, what we let "in" or what we let the world see. We live in fortresses to avoid vulnerability and weave our social lives around these pretenses, ultimately living not from our authentic self but from our safe and secure manmade refuge.

Pursuits, passions, drives are not wrong, but when misplaced as identity and security, they become stumbling blocks that keep us from living from our true, authentic selves. As the parable in Matthew 7 warns, a house built on sand will come crashing down, but a house built on rock will withstand the storms. Nelson and I had each built our identities on shifting sand, which crashed with the forces of change, transition, and hardship. We were left with a choice: will we rebuild the same walls or allow God to bring forth something new because we serve a God who makes all things new?

One particular afternoon, Nelson and I found ourselves on polar opposite ends of the counseling couch with an icy wind blowing between us. The night before we had argued bitterly about vices, habits, expectations, trust. I sat stone-faced and resentful in Dr. Hurley's office, wanting vindication that I was right and Nelson was wrong. In a moment of complete vulnerability and honesty, Nelson opened up. "It's me. I thought I had it together. I thought I was in control. I found comfort in those violent environments, but I was wrong. That's not who I am," Nelson humbly mumbled. "I have to find me again. All aspects of me."

Intense compassion washed over me. Here was a man who was willing to give up everything, including his reputation among Special Forces peers, to battle his inner wars. Swallowing hard, I let the tears fall.

Sensing the tension had softened in the room, Dr. Hurley allowed each of us to present our side of the argument. With kind eyes, Dr. Hurley turned to me and said, "Don't let getting your way be wrapped in your identity." *Ugh*, his words were truth arrows to the heart. In that moment, it was apparent my battle was not really against Nelson, but rather against myself, my three Ps, and the habits of my heart.

My prayer-chair homework was cut out for me when I got home. Getting my way was a hard roadblock to overcome. It was second nature to find the issues or weakness in an argument or case, and then push for my voice to be heard. Throughout my life, getting my way was a sign of success, a stamp of approval from others. Stemming from childhood and a competitive family, "being right" was tied to perfectionism, performance, and deep-rooted feelings of acceptance. My identity in being right was definitely linked to getting my way. This was about my heart, my push for perfection, my need to be right. In a humbled state, I started to pray for a right and true identity for both me and my husband:

I confess and repent, Lord, for allowing perfectionism, performance, and perception to be the voice in my head guiding me. I confess that I thought I could control myself and those around me by erecting these false facades. Take back all the areas of my heart that have been hurt by these false hiding places, and I ask You to exchange them for the one true Rock. Please, let Nelson and me taste the glory of Your peace, the safety of finding refuge in You alone, and restoration of our true identities.

It is right and true to take pride in our accomplishments and performances. It becomes wrong when they become twisted into our identity and who we are. It is right and true to love your children, but not when that love is twisted into our source of emotional comfort. It is right and true to seek to do your best in everything and to do it right, but not if it becomes who we are. All these "good" things became distorted in our lives, and the enemy was right there to pervert the truth, just as he did with Eve in the Garden. Our false selves, clothed in garments of pride, self-centeredness, jealousy, and fear, could not stand the force of the storms in marriage.

Under the scalpel of the Lord and with the help of counseling, Nelson and I each began to shed our false self. Trauma is difficult to treat because a person often develops survival tactics that can lead to a false self.[19] "On the outside, I was a hardened Green Beret, strong, trained, a leader of my men. But on the inside, I was always measuring myself. Everyone seemed to have it together, but I thought I didn't. I was the kid with big glasses. No matter my accomplishments, I still saw myself as the kid with big glasses. After a decade of oscillating between conflict zones—combat war and an unhealthy, insecure previous relationship—I buried my insecurities behind a strong exterior," Nelson reflected during another session.

When Nelson started to undergo EMDR and process his inner life, he was asked to relive each horrific scene and identify the deep feelings in the moment. "What came up every time was a lie spun to make me not believe in who I was. The lies were, I wasn't strong enough to save my comrades, I wasn't fast enough, I was weak, I was afraid," Nelson reflected, as he thought about the past. "All these lies were being whispered to me and that is what I lived out of and what carried me and pushed me to be stronger, faster, harder than anyone else. Magnify that with all the other traumatic events and they compound, so my identity became wrapped around lies."

"With everything I built crumbling around me, I don't know who I am anymore," Nelson confided again with Dr. Hurley. "I have come to the realization that I don't know who I am. Who am I? Who am I without God? This is where I am. I believe that these years of unguided, feeble attempts at being a 'man' have led me to this point in my life. I have been a man of this world, this flesh. Without God in my core, I have become toxic to myself and those around me."

Nelson did not know he was echoing the very lessons C. S. Lewis had learned: "It is no good trying to 'be myself' without Him. The more I resist Him and try to live on my own, the more I become dominated by my own heredity and upbringing and surroundings and natural desire."[20]

Thank goodness the God I serve does not want to pursue the person I've created myself to be, but the one He created and called into life. The God I serve does not love the Anne and Nelson we made ourselves to be, but the true and authentic selves He created us to be. God relentlessly pursues us, tearing down every wall that prevents Him from forming His likeness in us. The choice is up to us to resist Him or allow Him to usher in His wisdom, His grace, His heart.

No matter our worldly accolades, bravery, and abilities, it is our hearts and our identity that so easily bruise. Life's circumstances, the lemons thrown at us, the traumas endured, shape who we are and how we see ourselves. We think we "find ourselves" by overcoming hardships and difficult situations, divorce, abuse, or dysfunctional families. In reality, unless the victory over hardship is through the love of our Father and the work of Christ who transforms our hearts, we are simply "get-throughers."

Abba Father was chiseling our true identities from the rubble and clearing major roadblocks to restoration in the marriage. Ephesians 3:20 reminds us that our Father is able to do immeasurably more than all we *ask* or *imagine*. I have a huge imagination, and yet our Father is still bigger and has bigger plans for us within His purpose. But it's conditional on the extent we allow Him to work in our lives. Thankfully, our Abba Father relentlessly pursues His creation, and He allows circumstances in our lives to tear down the walls of false security and false self. If we resist this process by running to other false securities, we will live in bondage and remain stuck.

Standing Straight

Leanne Payne, in her book *The Healing Presence*, describes the posture of finding security and identity in other humans or false identities as being "bent" toward them.[21] She writes, "The drive to dominate, possess, or manipulate persons and things in order to meet our own needs taints (or replaces altogether) the healthy, satisfying relationships we are designed to have and by which we are to be nurtured."[22] By subjectively reacting to each other and attempting to control life and manipulate outcomes, Nelson and I were both bending into each other, intertwined like we were playing a life-sized game of Twister. In contrast, when living standing straight up and looking at the Creator—face toward heaven, arms stretched open—we assume the posture of full and true identity. It is a place of being filled from Creator and not the creation. Nelson and I were learning to unbend ourselves and seek the Father for all the areas exposed through our war.

As standing after from leaning over can cause a backache, similarly, as our spiritual posture straightened before the Lord, we felt our stiff heart muscles readjust. Daily, and sometimes even moment to moment, we had to choose to walk upright, in our right identity, and speak truth over ourselves. The enemy is waiting behind every fallen rock of our previous identities and strongholds to ensnare us.

Nelson shared the cry of his heart after one episode: "Our Father in Heaven . . . forgive us and cleanse us, Lord! Then clothe us in Your favor and protection, the ARMOR OF GOD!!! Why do I feel this way? I feel I am making progress, but when I do, the enemy attacks!!!! WHY???!!" The enemy goes to great lengths to steal what God blesses us with, including our identity and security. For if we never live life fully as who God created us to be, the enemy has succeeded in stealing our future.

The road to restoration, though, is slow, painful, and often two steps forward and three steps back. The enemy is always close by to whisper in our ears, scheming ways to pull us away from our true identity in God. The enemy comes to steal, kill, and destroy the works of God, with a particular focus on the identity of His children. We are God's children, created in His likeness for His purpose and His calling. We each have a unique calling to fulfill, and the enemy will do everything in his power to prevent us from living our fullest.

Self-condemnation rumblings in our heads give the enemy an open door to cheer us on, saying, "That's right, you are insufficient, incapable, a failure, unworthy," and the list could go on. But those names mean nothing when standing in the presence of the One who created us, redeems us, and calls us friend and worthy of His love. Like Eve, if we give the voice of the enemy a seat at the table, it can drown out the voice of our Creator. Ultimately, we have free will to choose to whom we will listen and from which table we will be fed.

Scripture, thankfully, is full of affirmations to counter the lies of the enemy and fight for our true identities: I am not unlovable, I am chosen and dearly beloved (Colossians 3:12); I am not without value, I am precious in His eyes (Isaiah 43:4); I am not invisible, I am seen and known and called by my Father (Jeremiah 1:5); I am not easily dispensable, I am accepted and treasured (Romans 15:7); when I am weak, then I am strong (2 Corinthians 12:10); I am not a mistake, I am fearfully and wonderfully made (Psalm 139); I am not a victim, vindication is my inheritance in the Lord (Isaiah 54:17).[23]

Memorizing and repeating these truths of Scripture helped anchor us to Christ and untwist our bent spirits. Leanne Payne describes the true self as "the self that abides in Christ and collaborates with Him."[24]

True and right identity cannot be shaken when rooted in the Creator, for we come from Him and in Him alone do we find ourselves. Jesus gave up all heavenly honor to be born a human, spat on and disregarded, shunned and scorned, and yet He remained confident of His identity as the Son of God and in His purpose on earth. And He has given us His assurances that the Spirit that empowered Him and raised Him from the dead is alive and lives in those who believe.

Nelson and I both needed our Creator to speak His affirmation to our hearts, to give us a renewed sense of purpose and direction. We were fighting for our identity, our true identity as children of God, as accepted by Him, loved by Him, known by Him. Being securely attached to our Creator ensures a true rock, fortress, and guide. Turning to God in the midst of our sickness and shame is the heart of spiritual transformation.

So together, in prayer, Nelson and I turned to the Father and asked Him who we were, clinging to the truth that our Creator calls us by name (Isaiah 43:1). That means He knows us, and asks for us, calling to us as He did Adam and Eve in the Garden, looking for us to walk with Him in the cool of the evening. Tuning our ears to the Holy Spirit, we waited for Him to softly speak to our hearts. Individually we wrote down what the Lord said on separate pieces of paper and then exchanged them. Quietly opening our papers, we paused in a moment of amazement. He had whispered the same word to us both: BELOVED.

Yes, that is who we are, that is our true identity. We are beloved children of the Most High God. We have His blessings, His protection, His heart.

CHAPTER EIGHT

CLEANING THE
THOUGHT TROUGHS

Men are not prisoners of fate, but only
prisoners of their own minds.
—Franklin D. Roosevelt

You have power over your mind – not outside events.
Realize this, and you will find strength.
—Marcus Aurelius

DAYS BECAME WEEKS, WEEKS BECAME months, and months became years, and slowly, like a snail running a marathon, we inched forward through the valley, our feet on the path of reconciliation. Counseling and EMDR helped set us on the road, but there was much work to do individually. There were still deep heart issues the Lord was uprooting and adjusting, so the path was littered with the boulders of our problems, reactions, and negative habits. There should have been a huge "Hazard! Construction Zone" sign swinging over us. During and after an episode or argument, spiraling thoughts of hatred, divorce, anger, and bitterness still often welled within me and spilled onto my tongue. Angry words, true but bitter-infused words were designed to sting, to cut through the episode and go straight for his heart.

Who have I become? Before Nelson, I had never yelled or full-on bellowed at another human. But now in my marriage it was commonplace, almost like an outlet. The "D word"—*divorce*—was my choice weapon to hurl, which had led to a hardening of our hearts toward each other. In my deep heart of hearts, I did not want a divorce, but feeling trapped and overwhelmed, I used fear to hurt him. Clenched fists and jaw, I would turn away from him and long for a different life, pleading, "Lord, heal Nelson's damaged and negative thought patterns."

Only as a gentle shepherd can do, as counseling sessions and mornings at His feet compounded, He started to show me an image of the well of my heart. The water was polluted and mucky, slimy, not potable. The heart is the well that catches the drips of our thoughts and from which the river of our words flow. Thoughts that dwell on the whys and woes, thoughts that focus on ourselves and the injustices we experience turn the well of our heart sour. As James 3:11 reminds us, fresh water and salt water cannot flow from the same fountain.

My water was salty. I needed the sweet, fresh water of Jesus to cleanse me. So much rot had led to negative thinking, moments of despair, feelings of helplessness, and verbal onslaughts against my husband. I soberly remembered the words of Jesus in Luke 6:45, that the mouth speaks what the heart is full of; our thoughts fill the cistern of our hearts from which our mouths speak. I had been asking the Lord to change Nelson's thoughts, but the Lord was asking me to take the log out of my own eye first. To fully become the persons God created me to be, I had to undertake the arduous task of cleaning my thought troughs

✦

You Are What You Think

Episodes were triggered by a thought, a fear, a word not rooted in the peace and confidence of Christ. Like a paperclip train, one thought led to another, invoking emotions, which translated into words and actions that caused significant arguments. Conflict ensued and deepened with every subsequent thought. Negative thought patterns established themselves in both of us, as Nelson's thoughts triggered reactive negative thoughts in me. It was a caustic cocktail.

Many a night after an episode fueled by self-righteousness, I would fall asleep with seething thoughts toward my situation and my husband. Condemning thoughts coursed through my mind, filling me with all the ways I was right and he was wrong. My mind was like a nonstop reel, evaluating actions, judgments, intentions, what I said or others said, the good and ugly mixing together, making the water murky. Drip, drip, drip went the bitter spring of my thoughts.

Mahatma Gandhi once said, "A man is but the product of his thoughts—what he thinks, he becomes." Be careful what you say to yourself; your thought habits will fill the well of your heart and bleed into your character and your actions. From Ghandi to the posters on school walls reciting ancient Chinese philosopher Lao Tzu,[25] we are warned to watch our thoughts for they become who we are. You are what you think. What we think has tremendous power over our lives.

Beliefs about ourselves or spouse that are unspoken still sit in the background of our thoughts, frame our vision and responses, and influence our interactions with people and with God. If I was what I thought, I was bitter, angry, resentful, and self-righteous. What I was living through justified my thoughts. To me, they were the normal response to the situation. But just because a situation or circumstance can legitimize a response does not mean it is the right response, the response required of God to be righteous.

I need you, Lord. I still get angry quickly and cut Nelson to the core with verbal onslaughts. Feelings of nastiness arise. I don't like how I respond and I need a miracle.

One Sunday, I found myself alone in church. Lingering in the pew, an older woman I barely knew startled me by touching my shoulder. "Would you like to join me for lunch?" she asked with a tinge of I-can-tell-not-all-is-well in her voice. "Sure, thank you, I would love that," I replied, happy for the company.

Sitting across from her at Applebee's, she told me she had been present when I asked about the anointing oil and had kept an eye on me from afar, praying from the pews, so to speak. She asked me if I would be willing to share my story. I gave the condensed version, focusing on what I was particularly struggling with at that moment: controlling my thoughts. Then my elderly friend kindly offered her own story:

"My dear, I had a long history of deep depression from abuse I endured as a child. The first forty years of my life I lived in the darkness. These last forty years I have lived in the light. Jesus miraculously healed me. I knew I was healed, but I had to walk out my healing.

"What did that look like?" I questioned, curious while really thinking of my own situation.

The woman with gray hair, soft skin, and direct eyes responded, "I would be driving down the interstate when my racing thoughts would try to dominate me, pulling me into a spiral of depressive thinking. Rather than let those thoughts win or allow the enemy to win because he knew I was on a tight time schedule, I would pull over on the shoulder, pull out my notepad, and write down every negative thought that was flooding my mind. Then on the next page, I would ask God what He thought of me, and I would write down every positive, affirming thought from God."

Her words flooded my mind. Was this the key I needed to help rewire my own thoughts and responses? Just as I learned to identify my feelings, I knew I needed to learn to weigh my thoughts on the scale of truth. When deeply wounded, our perspective on life comes from the injured mindset, and Satan will use it against us. I needed a way to overpower the boney finger of the enemy.

Heeding the advice of my wise gray-haired friend, I went home and began a thought-journal. I kept it close to me at all times. Pages and pages filled quickly. On the left side, laments, lies, anger, pain; and on the right side, truths found from the Truth Giver. "This is too much to handle," was replaced with "Jesus is all-sufficient and my burden bearer." "I can't forgive him for what he said last night" was replaced with "Jesus is the quieter of the storm." "I want to quit; I blew it again" was replaced with "Remember the Trinity unity and new mercies every morning."

Writing my thoughts became particularly powerful because it enabled me to physically remove the thoughts from my mind, put them on paper, and hand them to Jesus. Taking my thoughts captive on paper helped reorient my mind and to think about what was true, what was noble, what was lovely, what was pure, and what was praiseworthy (Philippians 4:8). When I heard something or felt something contrary to the words of Christ, I started to use my newly discovered authority to bind it and did not let it land—or tried to not let it land. It's a hard road of practice and repetition.

Lord, I confess my bitterness, my hardness, my anxious thoughts. I bind these thoughts and submit them to you. I take captive these negative feelings and thoughts, bind them as tools of the enemy to bring conflict. Replace the songs of cynicism with lovingkindness.

When a negative thought crested the waters in my mind, I squashed it with an encouraging verse, hymn, poem, or proverb. I memorized a few lines and put them on repeat until a negative thought was browbeat into submission. When hurtful words flew like bullets, I would repeat to myself a mixture of Scripture: "A calm and undisturbed mind and heart are the life and health of my body. God did not give me a spirit of timidity or fear, but a spirit of power and love, a calm mind, discipline, and self-control."

By keeping a thought-journal I started to track my thought patterns. What we say to ourselves—repetition of thought—shapes the reality we live in. Most of my negative thought patterns stemmed from a belief that life should be a certain way. I had developed wrong ways of thinking in response to the episodes, my own fears, and my own efforts of self-preservation. The journal revealed my habitual ways of thinking, which gave insight into specific areas that needed renewal through the truths of Scripture. My daily prayer became based on Psalm 139:24-25: "Search me and know me, Lord. Test my thoughts. Find any unclean thing in me and remove it." Changing our thought habits takes practice and time; it takes the daily renewing of the mind.

There is a reason the Lord says to not let the sun go down on your anger.[26] In the night, seeds of darkness grow dark thoughts. When we fall asleep thinking of all the reasons we don't like our spouse, or they don't deserve us, or we're better than them in some way or the other, those thoughts are little drips feeding negative seeds that take root deep in the night. Those seeds become weeds and strongholds onto which the enemy latches. The enemy has many millennia of experience tearing relationships apart, starting with thoughts to influence feelings and then actions.

My thoughts were more in line with the accuser of our souls. Negative thoughts and thought patterns opened me up to the enemy. I do not serve a God of negativity or a God who condemns. These thought patterns were fodder for the enemy, the one who points out my husband's faults and the faults of others. The enemy wanted more than anything for me to agree with his accusations. I had to choose not to come into agreement.

As Oswald Chambers says in *My Utmost for His Highest*: "Thoughts about myself hinder my usefulness to God."[27] I would add that thoughts about others also hinder our usefulness to God. My thoughts toward and about my husband were not a representation of Jesus in my life or his. It takes the grace of God to straighten the critical crooks in our path. Every day is a choice to stand in agreement with God that my husband is His masterpiece, being formed and shaped, covered by the blood of Jesus; or to stand with the accuser of my husband's soul and agree with his judgments over Nelson.

Change came when I took my mind's eye off reacting to Nelson and allowing the Lord to reorder my thoughts. God is always speaking, the question is whether I am tuned into His frequency, my own, frequency or the enemy's frequency. Learning to tune my ear to the Lord, to quiet the inner noise and mental marathons, was, and is, a slow, deliberate, and difficult endeavor. In many ways I am still living out my healing, as the enemy lurks behind every emotion to drag me back down. When tuned into the Lord, the fruit is evident. The voice of God brings life, the truth of God brings freedom and peace. Isaiah 26:3 promises that God will "keep him in perfect peace, whose mind is stayed on [Him], because he trusts in [God]" (NKJV). By bringing my thoughts into alignment with the truths of Scripture and the God of love, the path of restoration became a bit more level.

Bless, Do Not Curse

Our tongue is a weapon, and I had become very astute at using it to tear down my husband in order to build up myself. I would spew venomous words, feeling it was the only way I could express the jumbled feelings inside. I knew Nelson was hurting too. I knew his heart was crying out, but I allowed walls of resentment and bitterness to turn my heart cold toward him. The longer we argued and spewed venom at each other, the further disconnected we felt, and the more negative our interactions became.

Dr. Sue Johnson, in her book *Hold Me Tight*, describes the fighting Demon Dialogues—a fitting name for our words because they became arrows of the enemy to tear apart each other, our identity, and ultimately the relationship. "We either become demanding and clinging in an effort to draw comfort and reassurance from our partner, or we withdraw and detach in an attempt to sooth and protect ourselves."[28]

Nelson's demanding was his way of saying, "Need me. Make me feel safe and loved," while my detached response said, "I won't let you hurt me. I will chill out, try to stay in control."[29] I resolved to be strong, finding fortress in my previous ways of dealing with pain. We were each desperately holding tight to what was pushing the other away.

Round and round we went. The more I pushed for him to see the error of his ways, the more he retreated and spiraled. The more abusive his words became, the more I retreated and spiraled into a self-licking, self-righteous ice-cream cone. It was a vicious spiral. Even with all our tools and coping skills, our flesh and triggered responses won most often in the early days of healing. Blame and criticism triggered defensiveness, which led to smear campaigns and "demon dialogues."

I had taken a new teaching position in a Christian school where the main theme for the year was "Speak Life," based on Proverbs 18:21: "Death and life are in the power of the tongue, and those who love it will eat its fruit" (NKJV). This theme could not have come at a more opportune time. Day in and day out I was reminded to speak life to our students and for our students to speak life to each other, and that eventually seeped into my thinking about how I spoke to my husband at home.

Our words have meaning. Every word is either a blessing or a curse. Out of my mouth came both praising and cursing, which James 3:9 cautions against. My tongue needed to be bridled as my thoughts were being taken captive. With "speak life" ringing in my ears and the Scripture verse about blessing and not cursing each other, I sought the advice of the wise women at church. I simply asked, "How do I bless someone?" And the answer was surprisingly more simple than expected. The seasoned women in the group explained that by choosing to speak life to someone was blessing them. A blessing is speaking life over someone, speaking good of them—not ill, speaking the Father's heart toward them and not the enemy's.

Blessing an easy person is easy, but what about the one putting you through emotional abuse, verbal abuse, or even financial abuse? When our hearts want so badly to call down the wrath of God on someone but we choose to bless those who persecute us, it is another way of getting our will out of the way for God's will to be done. By speaking life, we call on God to see even our enemies with favor, to call them toward Him, to redeem them as He did us.

Speaking life is using our will through our words to declare *good* will toward someone, declaring truth over them—God's truth. I knew the areas where our hearts fumbled and needed reassurance. They were the areas I often targeted with my harsh words. The Lord quietly spoke to me, "Anne, turn those areas into puddles of life. Bless those areas."

Blessings can be Scripture personalized for someone or can be exhortations directing them to Truth, whether spoken to the person directly or in our hearts. The Lord sees our hearts and honors what we say.

Nelson, I bless you with strength and courage in the midst of the battle.

I bless you as an overcomer because your hope and safety are in the Lord.

I bless you with deep knowledge that Jesus will never leave you nor betray you.

One of the best resources I still use (though all worn) today, is the little booklet called *Daily Spirit Blessings* by Sylvia Gunter. Blessing our enemies, blessing those who curse you, is engaging in a spiritual battle and allowing the Holy Spirit to fight for us.

Choosing the act of blessing was choosing to lay down my verbal weapon and pick up my spiritual weapon; choosing to align my words with the thoughts of the Father. I may have started the blessing with clenched teeth, but inevitably it ended with a soft heart and renewed hope. I would read aloud from one of Gunter's entries:

> [Nelson,] I bless you with deep heart identity as God's very own child, securely loved in His family, calling him "Abba, dear Father." I bless you with the settled assurance that He has a future and a hope for your best interests and His ultimate glory. I bless you with deep knowledge that your Abba knows what you need and has all the resources of the universe to meet your needs. I bless you with confidence that you lack nothing and need in any way. I bless you with certainty that you are an heir with your brother Jesus to all your Father's treasures. I bless you in the name of the Spirit of sonship.[30]

It is not only important to put the enemy behind bars in your marriage, but equally as important to release blessing into it. I learned to bless our physical bodies, to bless our spirits, bless our home and all who stepped foot into our space, and most importantly, bless my husband. I started blessing even Nelson's socks as I folded them,

Anne W. Smith

his underwear, pants, and anything that would be part of his day.

Learning to bless was learning to call forth the good and the true, which opened the path for the Spirit to do His work in both our hearts. Blessing is another way of coming into alignment with the Kingdom of God rather than the accuser of our souls.

CHAPTER NINE

A (NEW) TEAM

I would rather walk with a friend in the
dark than walk alone in the light.
—Helen Keller

REDEPLOYING AFTER THE INITIAL INVASION of Afghanistan, Nelson was assigned a new team—the Triple Nickel, the most elite scuba team in all of the 5th Special Forces Group. Young, new, and eagerly trying to fit in on the team of seasoned Green Berets, Nelson was mortified when the colonel, who had been with him in Afghanistan, popped his head in the team room. Upon redeploying, Nelson had dragged his feet in getting a comprehensive medical assessment done. "Son, I am ordering you to have a medical evaluation immediately," the colonel stated.

Already embarrassed by being singled out by the colonel in front of the team, the medical evaluation provided more fodder for Nelson's internal shame and disgrace. Scans showed he was riddled with shrapnel, broken bones, and neck damage. (In fact for years afterward, Nelson's body would push out little pieces of metal; he often woke up laying on shrapnel shards.) He returned from the medical evaluation on crutches and in a neck brace.

While still in his defeated posture of crutches and a neck brace, Nelson was awarded a Purple Heart and a Bronze Star with the Valor Device for his courageous actions. Though an honor to have a Purple Heart, it was received with a red face. Standing in a field surrounded by trees, each planted in remembrance of a fallen brother— with fresh plantings from the men who died from the bomb— Nelson was pinned the two distinct awards. "What should have been a proud moment was covered in shame and embarrassment. Leaning on crutches, having the medals pinned to my neck brace was the most humiliating moment of my life," Nelson solemnly remembers. "I felt as though I did not deserve the awards. I was just doing what I was supposed to be doing anyway, and I did not want to be perceived as weak."

On a team, weakness is shunned, and being relegated to crutches and in a brace meant Nelson could not be an effective member. Teams will accommodate for only so long. "Being kicked off an A-Team you are sent to the B-team. No one wants to be on the B-team," Nelson explained. B-team guys are not action guys.

Nelson tried to pull his weight and get by without using the crutches, but then, ironically, the team sergeant threatened to remove him from the team if he did not stay on his crutches. Nelson was forced to come to terms with his situation and allow time to heal the wounds.

An A-Team is a stalwart force of brute strength and razor precision, with powerful currents that keep team guys in competition and in camaraderie. During Nelson's time, A-Teams (or Alpha Teams) only had *alpha*-males.[31] On a team it is a dog-eat-dog world. Team guys must project strength. If you show your jugular, they will go for it. There were only two options on a team: be the ideal team guy or get kicked off. Weakness was not tolerated. On the flip side of the same coin is a team that is bonded, that will fight and die together.

Special Forces troops undergo hours upon hours of psychological training to prepare them for combat and combat-related problems. They are highly trained, highly regulated soldiers. Individuals who successfully completed the rigorous Army Special Forces candidate school were significantly higher in personality hardiness than those who failed.[32] In other words, to even be a Special Forces soldier, these guys had to have great psychological resilience.

A study that screened only active-duty Special Forces personnel reported that SF guys had the lowest prevalence of mental disorders, physical health problems, and unhealthy behaviors. Team guys were approximately four times less likely to screen positive for any mental disorder than conventional forces infantrymen.[33] Nelson and his men were mentally and physically sharp, highly trained, highly resilient tips of the spear. They were warriors in every sense of the word.

However, team members are also less likely to report mental health problems or unhealthy behaviors than regular infantrymen.[34] These guys have it together, or so they project, embodying the culture of "get it together or get out." A sense of machismo runs deep among A-Teams. The stigma against getting help runs deep as well. There is a real fear that disclosing their symptoms might ruin their careers or reputations.

Teams do, however, hold a wild card, an X-factor that plays to the benefit of team guys, and that is the team itself. Shared pain, shared joys, shared missions, shared sorrows help a person be heard and known, and to cope. Nelson's A-Team operated as a brotherhood with shared combat, shared traumas, shared sorrows and joy. It was a temporary balm that kept the warriors ready to fight and not be oppressed by their experiences.

The twelve-man A-Team served as a tribe for these men. Their common language, experience, stresses, and hardships gave these men a place to cope with the constant business of war. Nelson admitted, "Until this point, I had held the belief that my fellow operators and I were relatively immune to the common effects of trauma. It never seemed to affect the team guys. After a violent engagement or a traumatic event, we'd openly talk about the day and events and move on. Sleeping wasn't a problem. We were calmer in a firefight than in a fight with our wives."

When warriors, however, step out of the arena that they lose their footing. The surface processing of the traumatic events within the safety of the team room served as a Band-Aid for many of these team members. But as these hardened warriors retire or part from the military, many lose the deep companionship that provided stability amidst the crisis they faced at home, at war, and within.

Leaving a team is like ripping these men from their safety zone. The team community serves as temporary balm to the wounds they carry. When the armor comes off and the team fades away, what is left standing is a hurting warrior who needs the deep embrace of the Healer, the One who held Nelson's heart in His hand through each battle, the One whose angels had thrown their arms around Nelson, shielding him from blast after blast. The cry of Nelson's heart exposed this sense of loss and confusion: "O Father, please help me. I am lost. At least I feel like I am. I need You, Your love. Please heal my brokenness."

When Nelson left the A-Team, he lost everything he had known. There is always a transition period, a time of adjustment. Help can come in many forms. Professional help was pivotal on the path to our healing, but just as important was finding a community, a new team, to walk with us.

Finding a Team

We are made for community. There has been a lot of talk the last few years about one's "tribe." A quick search on social media and you'll see an abundance of #mytribe connected to posts. Sebastian Junger wrote an entire book titled *Tribe: On Homecoming and Belonging* (Twelve, 2016). There is a deep-rooted desire to belong to a greater group, a team, to have a home within a larger entity. In today's modern societies where we often don't know our neighbors, where political differences are a source of neighborhood and even family fissures, and where we allow ourselves to be offended more easily than blessed by others, there is an even greater need for a larger collective group known as community.

As we walked the road of healing, it became crucial to discern with whom I shared our intimate needs and issues. I didn't want our issues to become gossip fodder, my thoughts to be affirmed only in an echo chamber, or to feed my own self-pity by seeking validation from others. Therefore, I shared and divulged only with those who met this criteria: they were willing and able to walk alongside me, uphold me with truth even if it was challenging to hear, and who saw my spouse and me as children of God, hurting and needing help.

The body of Christ is called to encourage, support, and uplift one another, to sharpen each other as iron sharpens iron (Proverbs 27:17). During our dark days on our path of restoration we were desperate for community, life-giving community. For too long we had been shamed into silence and isolated. Though we showed up to church on Sundays, no one knew our struggles. We felt unknown and unanchored. I was afraid of how people would respond if they knew the truth. I harbored anger and bitterness toward Nelson but was fiercely protective of his reputation. Deep in my spirit I knew he wasn't the man of the episodes, but how could I be sure others did not only see him as that?

"O Lord," I prayed, "bring the right people into our lives to guide us."

Providentially, Father Thomas started "formation groups" at church, which were like small groups but designed around spiritual formation practices. He arbitrarily chose each formation group, and each formation group required a commitment, a vow really, that we would meet every week; it was to be a priority in our lives. At first my husband resisted making the vow; we tend to be fly-by-the-seat-of-our-pants kind of people. Anchoring us to one commitment weekly was hard and uncharacteristic, but it turned out to be one of the best and most fruitful decisions.

We cautiously agreed, and each Tuesday evening we started to meet in the living room of John and Susan. Of course, there were evenings we wanted to run and not show up, but the commitment tethered us to the group, and we held to our duty. There were weeks when only I would show up, and the group knew without being told to pray a covering over us and Nelson, to call forth blessing on him and to remind us of the truths of a redeeming God.

Strict protocols shaped our time. We started with "check-ins," which involved no more than a two-minute update from each member on what they were bringing into the room that evening, but no one was allowed to engage or ask questions. This was not a time to discuss our problems. We each proverbially dumped our updates on the coffee table, placed them at the feet of the Cross, and asked the Holy Spirit to clear the room so He could work unhindered. We would then open with traditional evensong and spend an hour engaging in a spiritual discipline like lectio divina or ignatian contemplation. A safe space was created to allow the Holy Spirit to move in our respected lives.

Weekly, we engaged in confession, joined in congregational prayers prayed by the cloud of witnesses for centuries, and opened our hearts to the work of the Holy Spirit. The repetition, the liturgy of life, the rhythms that the formation group brought planted seeds that over time blossomed and brought forth healing and heart change.

Surrounded by a new team and opening Scripture through spiritual disciplines brought nourishment to the deepest parts of our souls—and new friendships. Friendships that saw the good in us that God created rather than stare at the ugliness we were overcoming.

One October Saturday afternoon, Nelson and I met up with another couple from the small group. We planned on going to the Oktoberfest festival to enjoy all things Bavarian. When we arrived, the scene was packed with party-goers. Looking for a place to sit and enjoy ourselves, we were swarmed by Lederhosen, hipster jeans, rowdy college students, and those who had had too much fun already. Nelson gripped my hand hard, his senses were on alert—and crowded spaces did not yield good outcomes. A train wreck was in the making. We stopped under a tent and looked at each other.

"Can we just leave?" Nelson asked, looking uncomfortable. I looked around, wanting both to honor my husband but also partake in the fun.

"Why don't we make our own fun? Let's get outta here. We can pick up some German beer and brats to grill at home in the backyard," our friends suggested. Under the care of friends who valued us more than an experience, we divided and conquered and by the end of the evening we were dining on bratwurst, homemade spaetzle, and Hacker-Pschorr. Crisis averted; hearts full.

Our new team, though different in form and function from Nelson's storied A-Team, loved us through our darkest days, without judgment. We were loved into healing. There is power in prayer, and even more power when many pray together. Second Corinthians 1:11 says there will be many thanks given "for the blessing granted us *through the prayers of many*" (emphasis mine). I am here today to give thanks for the blessing of a restored relationship through the prayers of many.

Being Vulnerable

It is hard to let friends, family, and neighbors see the ugly, to see how broken we really are or how messy our lives are. With an undercurrent that perception is reality, social media harnesses this deception: if I post the right pictures, if I dress a certain way, if I keep myself locked behind walls of performance, then no one will know I'm really a fraud and don't have it together. It is the most horrifying moment to have all your guts spill open in front of others. But it is the most beautiful and healing moment when those friends lean over and scoop up your mess and help put you back together.

Alone, we were vulnerable. The enemy would love nothing more than to pick off the lone ranger, the lone sheep. It is difficult to have and keep faith and ward off the accuser of our souls without others who can speak wisdom and truth into the fog. Only in bringing others into the pain and the problem will healing occur. By allowing others into our lives, we open the deepest parts of ourselves— exposing the good, the bad, and the ugly— and allow Christ's healing balm to be poured in. Without vulnerability, we deny the powerful working of the body of Christ.

In times of trouble, I often can't trust my own mind or heart; the lies of the enemy can swarm around me and cloud my thinking. During the hardest days, I would force myself to pick up the phone and let others into our mess. "Nelson's not in a good place," or "I'm not in a good place, please pray for us," I'd say. And you know what? The act of reaching out was met with an extended hand, a drop of the knee, and/or a word of wisdom.

It was the holiday season and our group was celebrating with a final group dinner. Nelson and I drove up and could see our friends already warm inside and getting the party started. We had been bickering on the ride over, but as we parked, the tension exploded. A full-blown episode erupted. I was in tears on the passenger side; Nelson was yelling at me from the driver's seat. Our small group leader came outside to wave us in. We motioned we'd be a few minutes. A few minutes turned into over an hour. Sadness and shame washed over us as we watched our small group take their seats around the beautifully set table, our seats remaining empty. How could we show our faces after this spectacle?

The episode simmered down but hurt and anger were now compounded by embarrassment. Together we got out of the car. Puffy eyes and heads bent low, we humbly rang the doorbell. John opened the door and without a beat welcomed us with a hug and a handshake, filling us in on what was being discussed at the table. We felt enveloped by their soft kindness and the absence of judgment or criticism. We were just loved. To be known and accepted, even with our masks off and the naked truth of our brokenness barred for all to see, brought immense healing to our souls.

Allowing others into our mess opened our hearts to healing, just as James 5:16 promises. We are to confess our sins to each other so that we may be healed. I believe that to confess does not just mean to tell others the big wrongs committed, but to tell one another our heart struggles, our heart attitudes, our hurts and deep wounds. Confession is coming into agreement that we need help; we can't survive by doing it alone. Limping into the group, we allowed our vulnerabilities to be exposed to the redemptive work of Christ through His body, the church, His A-Team.

⁘

Accepting Accountability

Anchoring to accountability is essential to pass through the storm, otherwise the siren call of self-pity, isolation, and depression can lead us to self-destructive acts. Knowing the siren call is inevitable, we must bind ourselves to the mast of Christ's truths spoken through our community. It is hard to ward off the accuser of our souls, the one who brings division, without others who can speak life and truth into the fog.

We let very few people in close to us during the digging-out stage. But those we did, we were confident they would minister to and with us. One such person was John, our small group leader. He and his wife had taken us under their wing, having us over for dinner often, calling and checking in throughout the week. We grew to respect their words and the wisdom that flowed through them.

One night as we were leaving their house, John, admonished us as we walked out the door, "Now go straight home, you two." We both thought that was a funny thing to say to grown adults. But we should have heeded his words. In retrospect, they were words from the Spirit telling us how to avoid pain and heartache. But instead, we decided to stop at one of our local spots to play shuffleboard and have a drink. Sure enough, something caught Nelson's thoughts and he started spiraling.

It could have been something as simple as me smiling at the bartender or watching a couple across the way. Regardless, it sent Nelson reeling and we proceeded to have one of the worst showdowns. Balled-up hearts and hurtful words took over, both of us slinging rocks with our words to hurt the other.

The Holy Spirit pre-warned us of dangers and pitfalls, giving us a way around, but our hearts were not in tune with His gentle guidance. That night we did not have ears to hear. Pride got the better of us, and as a result we backslid into self-destructive ways. Repenting to the Lord, He showed me Jesus' teachings, which often ended with Him saying, "He who has ears, let him hear."

"Oh, Lord," I responded, "open our ears. Give us eyes to see and ears to hear." The timeless words of Proverbs 19:20 instruct us to listen to advice and accept instruction that we may gain wisdom in the future. Whether the voice of the Holy Spirit or the reproof of respected leaders, the act of obedience and accountability free us from the cotton balls in our ears and release wisdom in our souls.

Our story could have ended in heartache and brokenness, but with the help of community, it ended in a stronger, deeper, more firm relationship. To the depth of my heart, I know we could not have made it through without the kindness, patience, and persistence of our church community and small group. The hands and the feet of Christ on this earth today is His church.

Vulnerability Is Hard

As the light dawned on our darkest of days, with our feet planted on the path of restoration surrounded by our small group companions, Nelson and I established one of the most important habits, which became a cornerstone

141

to our newly constructed marriage foundation: hospitality. We intentionally brought community into our home.

To help us rebuild together, to find common ground and share with others, we decided to follow another friend's example and start regular Sunday Suppers. Every Sunday evening we prepared a simple main course and invited others to join. Our weekly email read: "Bring yourselves, kids, neighbors, coworkers, travelers passing through, basically anyone who would like to join. You are welcome at our table. You can bring something, but you don't have to. The house will be messy. Comfy clothes are welcome. There might be games. There might be good Scotch, Filling Station beer, or a new wine to try. Come as you are. Arrive any time after 5:30 and leave when you must."

And people did come, and they left when needed. In the summers, we even had very pregnant women floating in the pool until 11:00 p.m.! Each week varied, with as few as six friends to as many as thirty, especially on warm-weather days.

The hand of God was evident as we never ran out of food—not once. Nelson and I would typically eat last, once everyone else got their food. One Sunday, however, I went to fill our plates but all of the platters were empty. "Nelson," I whispered, "we're out of food. Do you want me to make you a sandwich?" Just then Judy bounded through the door, almost skipping, with bags in her arms. "Sorry I'm late, you guys. I just felt like I should stop and grab something to bring," she exclaimed, as she pulled a huge tray of perfectly cooked shrimp and a giant Caesar salad from her bag. Jehovah Jirah, the God who provides, provided our favorite foods just when we thought we'd be eating scraps. Going to bed that night I could not help but see how God cares for us, provides and sustains us through His community.

Making the commitment to hospitality showed Nelson and me how to be gracious, real, and intentional, while allowing new sinews of tenderness to develop as we hosted friends, acquaintances, and strangers week in and week out. We could have been arguing all day or rebounding from an episode, but when friends arrived, it was like the wind of the Spirit brought new life into our home. It wasn't like we pretended everything was okay and put on a fake face, rather when we surrounded ourselves with people who loved us, who had seen the darkest days, they became the hands and feet of Christ in our home and the atmosphere shifted, tension was released, and the enemy had to flee in the presence of Christ's light.

These weekly gatherings became an enormous source of blessing and an obvious demonstration of being part of something bigger than ourselves. Our home was open, and our hearts were healing.

Leaning into community, hopefully an ever-expanding community, helps us learn to love one another and ourselves, as Christ commands. When we go beyond ourselves in asking and sharing, it helps us grow spiritually and emotionally. Remember the words of Paul in Hebrews 10:24-25: "Let us consider how to stir up one another to love and good works, not neglecting to meet together, as is the habit of some, but encouraging one another, and all the more as you see the Day drawing near."

No matter where you are, what situation you are in, if you look for Christ's community, it will find you. The first act of the fire of the Holy Spirit was to build up, encourage, and embolden the apostles to share the news of Jesus Christ. It brought thousands of people from different cultures, languages, races, and ethnicities together! The light of the Holy Spirit draws us into greater union with Him and each other. It unifies and ignites the fire in others for His name's sake.

An aspect of my job in Afghanistan was to help bring reconciliation between the government and tribes in remote areas. The first thing we often did was facilitate a *peace shura*, or a gathering of the elders and government officials to discuss and air grievances and forge a path forward. Each party had to listen to the other and hear the hurts before they could find common ground. The same principles apply everywhere, and even more so among Jesus followers. We are called, through the power of the Holy Spirit, to bring reconciliation and peace. We are called to love one another, to care for our neighbors. As Jesus people, we are called to weep with those who weep, to help the suffering and oppressed, and care deeply for all of God's image bearers. If we do not stand for reconciliation, repentance, and forgiveness, then who will?

The challenges we faced in overcoming our deep wounds, rebuilding ourselves, and rebuilding our marriage were made easier with the seasoned men and women who took us under their wings, speaking truth even when it was unpleasant. There is a spiritual battle for the hearts of people, a battle for unity, for identity, and for purpose raging all around us and within us. For such a time as this, the community of Christ is desperately needed. Together we call out for His Spirit, His light, to fall afresh on each of us.

Thank You, Lord, for bringing us community, for surrounding us with good friends, people who challenge and nurture us, and show us the church on earth.

CHAPTER TEN

HABITS OF THE HEART

Experiencing God will create a crisis of belief
that requires faith and action.
—Phyllis Crum

P RIOR TO INVADING IRAQ IN 2003, Nelson's team spent
days planning for every contingency, memorizing
grids and secondary grids, and knowing the
landscape and terrain. When the green light came, the
A-Team headed to the flight line where five Sikorsky MH-
53s waited to take them behind enemy lines. "The colonel
came down with the chaplain and sergeant major. The
chaplain never comes down, but everyone thought we
were going to die; we were the first to go in, and everyone
thought we would face chemical weapons," Nelson
thoughtfully explained.

The group of men gathered in a circle and the
chaplain prayed, then they all turned around and posed
for a picture. "We called it our 'death photograph.' The
colonel shook everyone's hands, then we half-hugged, got
in our Toyotas, and drove them onto the aircraft," Nelson
recalled. He sat in the back of the helicopter listening to
Linkin Park, waiting for the unknown to unfurl.

Just as Nelson's team did not know what they were going to experience when they landed in Iraq, we do not know what our marriages will produce when we say "I do." There are very few promises about the future and how it will turn out, but it *is* certain that in marriage we will face trials, hardships, hurts, and betrayal of varying degrees. In many ways, wedding pictures are our "death photos," an anchor memory, an anchor picture, a physical reminder of where the journey started.

Our journey started when our hearts found each other in a remote corner of the world. Together our hearts sang the same song, but each was dramatically out of tune. *Be patient with him, I am working on him* reverberated in the deepest part of my being, like a tuning fork. As Nelson neared retirement and prepared for civilian life, we continued to sort through our healing. The toughest days behind us, the Lord was still doing major renovations of our hearts, calling forth the real while tearing down the false.

As Nelson and I walked down the road of restoration, walking out our healing meant creating new ways to keep our hearts soft. Healing had to take place through reconciling with our past, traumas of war, the hurt we had flung at each other, but most importantly we needed to create new habits that bore positive fruit. Seeds die so a forest may sprout. A female salmon dies after birthing the next generation. Singlehood dies when two become one. An old self dies for a new self to be born. Death brings life. New habits will bring new fruit.

Faith, Hope, and Love

During our darkest nights, hope pulsing from my heart had to be the stronger force or despair could envelope me. My hope had to be in something outside of me, my situation, my control. The candle flame waned and flickered, nearly going out at times, but I planted my flag in the promises of Scripture, that He who started a good work is faithful to complete it, as Philippians 1:6 promises. I clung to the faithfulness of God, His promise to redeem and restore and make all things new.

I believe you, Lord, that you are doing a new thing, and calling forth new springs, new streams. In Christ, I am taken to the Father. As I hear Him, I am confident He will heal us and redeem us.

Hope, like oxygen, can't be seen or felt but is vital to our well-being and fuels confident expectation that the Lord will keep His promises. The habit of hope is more than an altruistic ideal, it is something that is qualitative, a nebulous idea that can be harnessed into actionable outcomes, and in the end produces something real, something tangible. Hope is a force that propels us forward to overcome obstacles that otherwise seem insurmountable.

As a follower of Jesus, my hope is in Him. Hope is real because Jesus is real. When our hope is built on anything else, it may fail us, but Jesus never will. Cling to His hope, for His hope will not disappoint. On this I am be assured, that when He is my cornerstone, my hope is secure. False hope, false identities, false refuges must be torn down so that Jesus can become the cornerstone. And on that rock I can place the weight of the world, the weight of my broken and messy situation, the hope of a future with love, joy and peace. Corey Russell, in his sermon "The Call to Return to Intercession," addressing the International House of Prayer, summarizes the importance of keeping our hope and faith on Jesus, who sits at the right hand of the Father:

> Do you keep going from trial to trial and whatever today's report is, that's what is going to govern yourself? Friend, we have got to begin to ascend to the throne of God. What does that mean? It means you say Bible verses, and you pray in the Spirit, and you begin to declare the truth, until . . . until the shift comes and you get there. What does that mean? When you get there, you'll know. In that place is peace, joy, righteousness and perspective.[35]

Lean into the Lord during times of refining for He is faithful and trustworthy. True change comes from the transformation of our hearts, not our circumstances. The hope in my heart had to be on the Rock of Ages, rather than in hoping my situation would change. I encourage you to ask the Lord for a Scripture or word of hope to get you through your own difficult season. Anchor yourself to that hope, knowing our God is faithful and true to His promises.

Even greater than faith and hope is love. Love is the hardest thing we can do on this earth. God gave His greatest commandment in Deuteronomy 6:5, that we are to "love the LORD your God with all your heart, and with all your soul, and with all your might" (RSV). Jesus added in Mark 12:30-31 that we must also love our neighbors as ourselves.

We live in a world where *self* is most important— self-service, self-promoting, selfies, self-awareness, self-esteem, self-love. The cross of Christ shows us that true love, however, is void of self—it is self-*less*. Without the power of the Holy Spirit, we are slaves to self and all its needs and desires.

Marriage is so hard. Loving someone is so hard. Lord, help me overcome me.

Love is a habit of the heart. It is the choice to have a posture of the heart toward our Creator, toward all He commands of us and asks of us. Accordingly, then, how I love others is a reflection of how I love God. How I love my spouse is a reflection of how I love God. The prevailing storms in our dark days revealed more about me than my husband: the habits of my heart were not loving; I was not patient; I was not kind; I envied; I kept records of wrong; I was easily angered. Christian marriage, Christian relationships, Christian community is meant to be a witness for Jesus and His love for us. Only through this sacrificial love— giving up my selfish ambitions and desires—could I be truly loving in marriage.

Forgive and Be Forgiven

Even after the ground under our feet grew more solid and Nelson and I were walking the road of restoration, a deep lack of forgiveness lingered in my heart. Despite the progress made on that long road, there were still moments when peace felt fleeting. Days, or even weeks, might pass without an episode, creating the illusion of reaching a lasting destination. But then, something would trigger a landslide, and the calm would be shattered once again.

The last two days were rough. Nelson's episodes lasted longer than the new normal. It exposed things in me, Lord. It exposed that I can still shut down my feelings quickly, that resentment is right there waiting at the door, and that my heart grows cold. How does one forgive?

A dear friend, Bethany, works with former child soldiers and children of war to bring them into peace and fullness of life through Jesus Christ. We became natural friends with a shared passion for international communities, and she, too, had gone through a difficult marriage. One warm summer afternoon, we went for a walk around Radnor Lake in Nashville. Talking about EMDR, counseling, community, faith, and all that was part of our story, I honestly confessed, "Bethany, I am not sure how to forgive Nelson even though we are on more solid ground now. I just don't know what that is supposed to look like or feel like."

She stopped walking, put her hand on my shoulder, and told me about a woman she had met on her travels to Rwanda. This woman, a survivor of the Rwandan genocide, had learned to forgive her enemy when she realized it was the evil within the man that did the killing and not the man himself.[36]

"One the reverse side," Bethany continued, "a boy named Ishmael was forced to commit unthinkable atrocities on his own community. When I asked him the greatest difference between who he was as a child soldier and who he was today, he responded, 'I had someone to believe in me. My adopted mother saw within me my humanity. She did not see what I had done; she saw what I could become.'"[37]

We stood there with the lake lapping in the distance, pondering what it meant to both forgive and be forgiven. I was convinced that seeing the humanity in our accuser, our persecutor, or the "other" is choosing to see what God sees and what God sacrificed His all to call His own. Forgiving and being forgiven sets captives free.

Home after the walk with Bethany, I pulled out my journal and Bible and asked the Lord to help me know what forgiveness in my marriage should look like or feel like. Sitting in silence for a few minutes, waiting on the Lord, He calmly spoke to my heart: forgiveness is not a feeling but a state of being. Forgiveness is an act of the heart, a habit of the heart, empowered by Jesus. Something the Winships taught me when in the Middle East came racing back—forgiveness is an accounting term; it means to cancel the debt owed you. As the rich ruler canceled the debt of his servant in Matthew 18, we, too, are to cancel the debt of what we feel or think others owe us, even if what we think and feel is justified.

> *Lord, help me to bear much fruit with wisdom and grace that come from you. I struggle to forgive Nelson; help me to forgive. I feel he "owes" me something—owes me apologies, repentance, and penitence. Help me be like the kind ruler who released the debt of his servant. Help me to release the debt I feel Nelson owes me. Lord, have mercy; Lord, have mercy; Lord, have mercy.*

Forgiveness is not celebrated in our culture because it violates our sense of fairness and desire for revenge. Pride whispers, "I am owed something. I am in the right. I am the hurt one." Forgiveness is a conscious decision to turn away from demanding what is owed us. Holding the debt—demanding reparations for pain acquired— is the root of unforgiveness. This does not mean legal consequences for legal grievances should not be pursued, rather, it means we do not harbor ill or self-service in our hearts toward the perpetrators. Even if retribution in the physical world has been repaid, not forgiving keeps us chained to the other, neither one free to live their best self.

When we do not forgive, we remain bound to the person we are not forgiving, like the gruesome punishment of ancient days when a prisoner would be chained to a corpse and forced to drag a putrefying dead man around. Choosing to not forgive ushers in bitterness and resentment and inner poison and will turn the heart cold and lifeless.

The heart of Jesus' ministry, however, was forgiveness. He ultimately was crucified so that our broken relationship with the Father could be forgiven and repaired. By His wounds we are healed, through forgiveness we are healed, therefore we must offer forgiveness in return. We are required to "make allowance for each other's faults, and forgive anyone who offends you. Remember, the Lord forgave you, so you *must* forgive others" (Colossians 3:13, NLT, emphasis mine). Forgiveness is so vital that Jesus says in Matthew 6:14-15 that if we are not willing to forgive, then the Father will not forgive us. When we do not forgive, we separate ourselves from God and each other.

One summer day, four years after all darkness had descended upon us, three years after I had hit rock bottom, I opened my heart to forgive. Taking a fresh piece of paper, I wrote down all the ways Nelson had hurt me, the ways I felt betrayed, the expectations I had for him making it up to me, the demands I had made on him soaked in my own pain, and the ways that I had hurt him and our marriage.

Calling him over, I slowly read each line. There was silence for a moment and I looked up, tears in my eyes, and said, "I release you from this debt. I forgive you. Will you forgive me for how I wronged you in my responses and in my pain?"

As one soft heart cried, the other responded in kind. Nelson took my paper and started jotting down the ways he needed to forgive and be forgiven. Together, we embraced, our hearts beating together in right rhythm. Taking the paper, I crumbled it up, lit a match, and we watched it burn into nothing but ashes. Isaiah 61:3 came to mind: "to grant to those who mourn in Zion— to give them a beautiful headdress instead of ashes, the oil of gladness instead of mourning, the garment of praise instead of a faint spirit; that they may be called oaks of righteousness, the planting of the LORD, that he may be glorified."

Nelson needed forgiveness, but so did I. Often the hardest person to forgive is ourself. I also had to forgive myself for how I acted toward Nelson, what I said to him in anger or hurt, and how I responded to episodes. I personalized a William Barclay prayer:

> *I forgive myself for everything I have done that has spoiled my relationship with Nelson. For the moodiness and irritability that has made me difficult to live with. For the insensitivity that has made me careless of the needs and feelings of my husband. Father, forgive me.*

Reconciliation started in my heart, learning to accept myself and forgive myself and then Nelson. It took an act of will to not let our worst moments mark our identities and prevent forgiveness. The enemy wants nothing more than to point his boney accusing finger and remind me of all my faults and shortcomings. But we serve a God who is quick to forgive and who looks at the depth of my soul and calls forth what He created in His image. No matter how much we mess up, our errors do not change the design God created for each of us.

The beauty of forgiveness is that it operates outside of time; it can be retroactive, healing our past and the present. Forgiving your past heals the memories, like EMDR in the physical realm. Forgiveness goes to the precise sore spots in the heart realm. Forgiveness is what realigns our head and our heart and enables them to work in unity. Forgiveness releases the prisoners and enables us to see the other as God created them. Sin and despair do not get the final say in the face of forgiveness.

Changed

Vibrant colors painted the May evening sky as a warm Southern California wind blew across our faces. Upon retiring from the Army, we said farewell to Nashville and moved to California for Nelson's new job. We silently surveyed our new home. The backyard was dust, boxes piled high along every wall, and we did not know a soul, but we were not worried. Our God makes streams in the desert! My belly was swollen with the anticipation of twin girls due any day. Nelson grabbed my hand and squeezed it tightly. We smiled at each other. It was our five-year anniversary. We had made it out of the valley. The sun was shining and new life beginning.

Thank you for redeeming us, for lifting us out of the pit, for washing us in Your blood, for calling us by name.

There was no instant, miraculous healing in our marriage or in our own hearts. But ever so slightly, ever so slowly, ever so intentionally we both were changed by the Holy Spirit, counseling, and community. Like early spring mornings when all of a sudden you wake up and realize it's light out now, the sun slowly but surely will rise and cast the darkness away. As God graciously put the pieces back together, our foundation was strengthened by heavenly steel beams. Struggle, pain, and death brought forth a stronger, more prolific essence, and what emerged became a life more beautiful than anything I could construct on my own.

Ground zero for conflict resolution starts in the heart with love, then in the home with forgiveness, then in our communities by collectively remembering the works of our Lord. The Prince of Peace took our transgressions on Himself that we may be healed—healed from broken relationships, healed from false refuges, healed from the wounding of others. *Healed*. Nelson and I were healing, in recovery, and reordering our systems and relationship away from fight, flight, or freeze. It was a long path, slow and arduous, with many, many more years of walking out our healing. But when we allow His Spirit access to our wounds, He will do His thing—heal and make new.

Whether or not you are in the middle of the storm or if your story ended differently than mine, the truths and promises of Christ to walk with you, teach you, forgive and redeem stand firm. He will lead you into and through the valley of death. He will be with you in the recalibration.

I prayed to the LORD, and he answered me.
He freed me from all my fears.
Those who look to him for help will be radiant with joy;
no shadow of shame will darken their faces.
In my desperation I prayed, and the LORD listened;
he saved me from all my troubles.
For the angel of the LORD is a guard;
he surrounds and defends all who fear him.
Taste and see that the LORD is good.
Oh, the joys of those who take refuge in him! . . .
Turn away from evil and do good.
Search for peace, and work to maintain it. . . .
The LORD hears his people when
they call to him for help.
He rescues them from all their troubles.
The LORD is close to the brokenhearted;
he rescues those whose spirits are crushed.
Psalm 34:4-8, 14, 17-18, NLT

* * *

ACKNOWLEDGMENTS

It was January 2021, on the eve of hosting the first "Declaration Dinner" at our home, when the Lord asked me to write what is now this book and declare it. Declaration Dinners, which have since become a cherished tradition, are fun, fancy parties where we gather friends to celebrate and declare our New Year's resolutions. At these dinners, we share what is on our hearts and what we hope to accomplish in the upcoming year(s), creating a supportive and festive environment to encourage each other in our endeavors. On the snowy, wintery night I stood among friends and declared I was going to write a book, not because I had anything to say, but because I wanted to obey the Lord's nudge. Three years later, a fourth baby, a move, many dirty diapers, nap times, temper tantrums (not just from the kiddos), and longs nights, I can honestly say, "It takes a village." I am so blessed to be surrounded by amazing friends from all ages and stages of life who have encouraged me every step of the way. Thank you!

There are a few close friends who walked this stretch of road with me and should be individually recognized.

First and foremost, without the love, support, encouragement, and bravery of my husband, our story and this book would not exist. Nelson, my heart you carry and hand you hold through the mountains, valleys, streams, and springs. You are a true man of God, a warrior, a visionary, a giver.

To my children, who gracefully suffered through many hours of being nursed in one hand while I typed with the other, or toddling around papers strewn across the floor, or playing at my feet to the soundtrack of typing, you fill our quiver; you are a blessing. May you never know a day apart from our Lord.

Mom, you never once gave up hope on Nelson, despite the crying, yelling, and frustration your daughter exhibited over the phone. You did not let my emotions change your resolute belief that there was a better plan for us. All the encouraging tips and tools of the trade you provided in the heart of battle ring in my ears to this day.

There is a wide and deep Nashville crew with whom much of our story is woven together. Laura McKenzie, godmother to our babies, we feel your ever-present prayers. Your love keeps Thomas's light alive and shining brightly. Our Formation Group—Judy, Linda, Hilary and Griff, Monica and Daniel, John and Susan, and Heather, you loved us into healing without judgment. Truly being the hands, feet, and heart of Christ, we thank each of you for your part in our story. Bethany and Matthew, thank you for walking with us through the valley and into the light of new life, for being the ones to introduce us to EMDR and what it looks like to overcome PTSD and bring others into the same hope. Glory to the Father who brought new life to us both in so many unimaginable ways!

Willingness to read early drafts of a manuscript is a mark of a true friend! Dad and Karen, our hours of conversation, contemplation, and counsel inspired me to turn the first draft inside out. Thank you for helping me see the forest for the trees. Christa, your deep knowledge of Scripture helped shaped numerous thoughts. Emily and Tres, I'll take any feedback with you over giant-sized pizzas and campfires. Your thoughts on voice and discernment informed hours of edits and rewrites! Luzon and Allison, you are the best closers. Your similar thoughts and impressions gave me fresh insight and the much-needed final touches. Every one of your time, talents, and feedback were paramount to helping me shape this story.

I would not be where I am today on my path to Christ if it were not for Phyllis, my fearless and fierce mentor who knows just when to give the wire-brush, soothing word, or exhortation. May my flash-to-bang be ever quickening, and my thirty seconds always steady.

To the Fire Mission and Declaration Dinner group, thank you for keeping me accountable and supporting me through prayer and parties!

And a big thank you to Westbow Press and my editor, Nancy Nehmer, for giving ordinary people like me a platform to share their stories of God's goodness and faithfulness.

APPENDIX A: PRAYING GOD'S PROMISES

The promises of God are powerful reminders of His faithfulness and lovingkindness. Below are just a few of the promises I clung to as we travailed through the valley of shadows. This is *not* an exhaustive list! Read each verse and then personalize it, sending your thunder bolt back into heaven (see page 59)! For a more in-depth study, a terrific resource is Beth Moore's book *Praying God's Word Day by Day* (B&H Publishing Group, 2006).

The LORD will fight for you; you need only to be still. Exodus 14:14, NIV

It is the LORD who goes before you. He will be with you; he will not leave you or forsake you. Do not fear or be dismayed. Deuteronomy 31:8

Even though I walk through the darkest valley, I will fear no evil, for you are with me; your rod and your staff, they comfort me. Psalm 23:4, NIV

I will instruct you and teach you in the way you should go; I will counsel you with my eye upon you. Psalm 32:8

The LORD makes firm the steps of the one who delights in him; though he may stumble, he will not fall, for the LORD upholds him with his hand. Psalm 37:23-24, NIV

Where shall I go from your Spirit? Or where shall I flee from your presence? If I ascend to heaven, you are there! If I make my bed in Sheol, you are there! If I take the wings of the morning and dwell in the uttermost parts of the sea, even there your hand shall lead me, and your right hand shall hold me. Psalm 139:7-10

The LORD is near to all who call on him, to all who call on him in truth. Psalm 145:18

You keep him in perfect peace whose mind is stayed on you, because he trusts in you. Isaiah 26:3

Fear not, for I am with you; be not dismayed, for I am your God; I will strengthen you, I will help you, I will uphold you with my righteous right hand. . . . For I, the LORD your God, hold your right hand; it is I who say to you, "Fear not, I am the one who helps you." Isaiah 41:10, 13

When you go through deep waters, I will be with you. When you go through rivers of difficulty, you will not drown. When you walk through the fire of oppression, you will not be burned up; the flames will not consume you. Isaiah 43:2, NLT

"No weapon forged against you will prevail, and you will refute every tongue that accuses you. This is the heritage of the servants of the LORD, and this is their vindication from me," declares the LORD. Isaiah 54:17, NIV

For I know the plans I have for you, declares the LORD, plans for welfare and not for evil, to give you a future and a hope. Jeremiah 29:11

Come to me, all you who are weary and burdened, and I will give you rest. Take my yoke upon you and learn from me, for I am gentle and humble in heart, and you will find rest for your souls. Matthew 11:28-29, NIV

The thief comes only to steal and kill and destroy. I came that they may have life and have it abundantly. John 10:10

I have said these things to you, that in me you may have peace. In the world you will have tribulation. But take heart; I have overcome the world. John 16:33

. . . casting all your anxieties on him, because he cares for you. 1 Peter 5:7

I can do all things through him who strengthens me. Philippians 4:13

If any of you lacks wisdom, let him ask God, who gives generously to all without reproach, and it will be given him. James 1:5

If we confess our sins, he is faithful and just and will forgive us our sins and purify us from all unrighteousness. 1 John 1:9, NIV

APPENDIX B: LIST OF EMOTIONS/FEELINGS[38]

Vocabulary of Emotions/Feelings

tomdrummond.com

Strong

Happiness	Caring	Depression	Inadequate	Fear	Confusion	Hurt	Anger	Loneliness	Remorse
Delighted	Adoring	Alienated	Blemished	Appalled	Baffled	Abused	Affronted	Abandoned	Abashed
Ebullient	Ardent	Barren	Broken	Desperate	Befuddled	Aching	Belligerent	Black	Debased
Ecstatic	Cherishing	Beaten	Crippled	Distressed	Chaotic	Anguished	Bitter	Cut off	Degraded
Elated	Compassionate	Bleak	Damaged	Frightened	Confounded	Crushed	Burned up	Deserted	Delinquent
Energetic	Crazy about	Dejected	Feeble	Horrified	Confused	Degraded	Enraged	Destroyed	Depraved
Enthusiastic	Devoted	Depressed	Finished	Intimidated	Flustered	Destroyed	Fuming	Empty	Disgraced
Euphoric	Doting	Desolate	Flawed	Panicky	Rattled	Devastated	Furious	Forsaken	Evil
Excited	Fervent	Despondent	Helpless	Paralyzed	Reeling	Discarded	Heated	Isolated	Exposed
Exhilarated	Idolizing	Dismal	Impotent	Petrified	Shocked	Disgraced	Incensed	Marooned	Humiliated
Overjoyed	Infatuated	Empty	Inferior	Shocked	Shook up	Forsaken	Infuriated	Neglected	Judged
Thrilled	Passionate	Gloomy	Invalid	Terrified	Speechless	Humiliated	Outraged	Ostracized	Mortified
Ticked pink	Wild about	Grieved	Powerless	Terror-stricken	Startled	Mocked	Provoked	Outcast	Shamed
Turned on	Worshipful	Grim	Useless	Wrecked	Stumped	Punished	Seething	Rejected	Sinful
Vibrant	Zealous	Hopeless	Washed up		Stunned	Rejected	Storming	Shunned	Wicked
Zippy		In despair	Whipped		Taken-aback	Ridiculed	Truculent		Wrong
		Woeful	Worthless		Thrown	Ruined	Vengeful		
		Worried	Zero		Trapped	Scorned	Vindictive		

Medium

Happiness	Caring	Depression	Inadequate	Fear	Confusion	Hurt	Anger	Loneliness	Remorse
Aglow	Admiring	Awful	Ailing	Afraid	Adrift	Belittled	Aggravated	Alienated	Apologetic
Buoyant	Affectionate	Blue	Defeated	Alarmed	Ambivalent	Cheapened	Annoyed	Alone	Ashamed
Cheerful	Attached	Crestfallen	Deficient	Apprehensive	Bewildered	Criticized	Antagonistic	Apart	Contrite
Elevated	Fond	Demoralized	Dopey	Awkward	Puzzled	Damaged	Crabby	Cheerless	Crestfallen
Gleeful	Fond of	Devalued	Feeble	Defensive	Blurred	Depreciated	Cranky	Companionless	Culpable
Happy	Huggy	Discouraged	Helpless	Fearful	Disconcerted	Devalued	Exasperated	Dejected	Demeaned
In high spirits	Kind	Dispirited	Impaired	Fidgety	Disordered	Discredited	Fuming	Despondent	Downhearted
Jovial	Kind-hearted	Distressed	Imperfect	Fretful	Disorganized	Distressed	Grouchy	Estranged	Flustered
Light-hearted	Loving	Downcast	Incapable	Jumpy	Disquieted	Impaired	Hostile	Excluded	Guilty
Lively	Partial	Downhearted	Incompetent	Nervous	Disturbed	Injured	Ill-tempered	Left out	Penitent
Merry	Soft on	Fed up	Incomplete	Scared	Dizzy	Maligned	Indignant	Leftover	Regretful
Riding high	Sympathetic	Lost	Ineffective	Shaky	Foggy	Marred	Irate	Lonely	Remorseful
Sparkling	Tender	Melancholy	Inept	Skittish	Frozen	Miffed	Irritated	Oppressed	Repentant
Up	Trusting	Miserable	Insignificant	Spineless	Frustrated	Mistreated	Offended	Uncherished	Shamefaced
	Warm-hearted	Regretful	Lacking	Taut	Misled	Resentful	Ratty		Sorrowful
		Rotten	Lame	Threatened	Mistaken	Tortured	Resentful		Sorry
		Sorrowful	Overwhelmed	Troubled	Misunderstood	Troubled	Sore		
		Tearful	Small	Wired	Mixed up	Wounded	Spiteful		
		Upset	Substandard		Perplexed		Testy		
		Weepy	Unimportant		Troubled		Ticked off		

Light

Happiness	Caring	Depression	Inadequate	Fear	Confusion	Hurt	Anger	Loneliness	Remorse
Contented	Appreciative	Blah	Dry	Anxious	Distracted	Annoyed	Bugged	Blue	Bashful
Cool	Attentive	Disappointed	Incomplete	Careful	Uncertain	Let down	Chagrined	Detached	Blushing
Fine	Considerate	Down	Meager	Cautious	Uncomfortable	Minimized	Dismayed	Discouraged	Chagrined
Genial	Friendly	Funk	Puny	Disquieted	Undecided	Neglected	Galled	Distant	Chastened
Glad	Interested in	Glum	Tenuous	Goose-bumpy	Unsettled	Put away	Grim	Insulated	Embarrassed
Gratified	Kind	Low	Tiny	Shy	Unsure	Put down	Impatient	Melancholy	Hesitant
Keen	Like	Moody	Uncertain	Tense		Rueful	Irked	Remote	Humble
Pleasant	Respecting	Morose	Unconvincing	Timid		Tender	Petulant	Separate	Meek
Pleased	Thoughtful	Somber	Unsure	Uneasy		Touched	Resentful	Withdrawn	Sheepish
Satisfied	Tolerant	Subdued	Weak	Unsure		Unhappy	Sullen		
Serene	Warm toward	Uncomfortable	Wishful	Watchful		Used	Uptight		
Sunny	Yielding	Unhappy		Worried					

167

Notes

CHAPTER ONE

1   Adam D. Cooper et al., "Mental Health, Physical Health, and Health-Related Behaviors of U.S. Army Special Forces," *PloS One* 15 no. 6 (2020). doi: 10.1371/journal.pone.0233560.

CHAPTER TWO

2   Jaquelle Crowe, "Put Jealousy to Death," Open the Bible with Pastor Colin Smith, August 22, 2017, https://openthebible. org/article/put-jealousy-to-death/#:~:text=We%27re%20 told%20that%20jealousy,(Romans%201%3A29).

CHAPTER THREE

3   Oswald Chambers, *My Utmost for His Highest* (Westwood, NJ: Barbour and Company, 1935), 153.
4   C. S. Lewis, *The Voyage of the Dawn Treader* (New York: Harper Trophy, 1980), 115–116.
5   Chambers, *My Utmost for His Highest*, 99.

CHAPTER FOUR

6   Anne Graham Lotz quoting Eugene Petersen, The Family Leadership Summit, July 11, 2016, 10:50 to 11:05, https:// www.youtube.com/watch?v=otpXIHud_kU.

CHAPTER FIVE

7   Chambers, *My Utmost for His Highest*, 98-99, 128-129, 136-137, 202.

8   Susie Larson, *Your Beautiful Purpose* (Minneapolis, MN: Bethany House Publishers, 2013), 93.

9   Leanne Payne, *Restoring the Christian Soul through Inner Healing Prayer* (Grand Rapids, MI: Baker Books, 1991), 46.

CHAPTER SIX

10   Francine Shapiro, *Getting Past Your Past: Take Control of Your Life with Self-Help Techniques from EMDR Therapy* (New York: Rodale, 2012), 138.

11   Shapiro, *Getting Past Your Past*, 135.

12   Ibid.

13   Ibid, 5.

14   "Eye Movement Desensitization and Reprocessing (EMDR) Therapy," American Psychology Association (APA), last modified July 31, 2017, https://www.apa.org/ptsd-guideline/treatments/eye-movement-reprocessing.

15   E. C. Hurley, "Effective Treatment of Veterans With PTSD: Comparison Between Intensive Daily and Weekly EMDR Approaches," *Frontiers in Psychology*, vol. 9 (Aug 2018): doi.org/10.3389/fpsyg.2018.01458.

16   Shapiro, *Getting Past Your Past*, 31.

17   Ibid.

18   "What Is EMDR—For Clinicians" EMDR Institute, Inc. Accessed June 2024, https://www.emdr.com/what-is-emdr/.

CHAPTER SEVEN

19   Judith MacNutt, "Trauma and Inner Healing" (presentation, Awake My Soul Conference of Galilee Episcopal Church, Virginia Beach, VA, March 22-23, 2019).

20   C. S. Lewis, *Mere Christianity* (New York: Harper One, 1980), 225.

21 Leanne, Payne, *The Healing Presence: Curing the Soul through Union with Christ* (Grand Rapids, MI: Baker Books, 1995), 59–68.

22 Payne, *The Healing Presence*, 60.

23 From my dear friend Christa's heart and prayers.

24 Payne, *Restoring the Christian Soul*, 26.

CHAPTER EIGHT

25 Watch your thoughts, they become words; words become actions; actions become habits; habits become your character.

26 Ephesians 4:26.

27 Chambers, *My Utmost for His Highest*, 251.

28 Sue Johnson, *Hold Me Tight* (New York: Little Brown Spark, 2008), 31.

29 Ibid.

30 Sylvia Gunter, "Day 5," in *Daily Spirit Blessings* (Birmingham: The Father's Business, 2005), adapted from Sylvia Gunter and Arthur Burk, *Blessing Your Spirit* (Birmingham: The Father's Business, 2005).

CHAPTER NINE

31 Since Nelson's retirement, Special Forces teams are now also open to females.

32 P. T. Bartone et al., "Psychological Hardiness Predicts Success in US Army Special Forces Candidates," *International Journal of Selection and Assessment*, January 25, 2008: 78–81, https://doi.org/10.1111/j.1468-2389.2008.00412.x.

33 Cooper et al., *Mental health, Physical Health, and Health-related Behaviors of U.S. Army Special Forces*, PLoS One, June 3, 2020, doi: 10.1371/journal.pone.0233560.

34 Ibid.

CHAPTER TEN

35 Corey Russell, "The Call to Return to Intercession," International House of Prayer, Kansas City, September 29, 2021, https://m.youtube.com/watch?v=i4uUcyexfpQ.

36 Read the whole story in Bethany's book *The Color of Grace*. Bethany Haley Williams, *The Color of Grace* (New York: Howard Books, 2015), 25.

37 Williams, *The Color of Grace*, 260.

APPENDIX B

38 Tom Drummond, "Emotion/Feeling Vocabulary," Tom Drummond-Resources&Writings,September8,2022,https://tomdrummond.com/leading-and-caring-for-children/emotion-vocabulary/.